PIVOT

The Nontraditional J.D. Careers Handbook

*Inspiring Stories and Practical Tips
for Lawyers Making Bold Moves
within the Legal Industry*

ALEXANDRA MACEY DAVIS, ESQ.

For Jacob, James, and Liam

PIVOT

Table of Contents

Introduction

I'll never forget how I felt on the afternoon of July 29, 2015: the end of the second and final day of the North Carolina Bar Exam. I slammed my laptop shut and stepped out of the aggressively air-conditioned testing center into the July sun. It was like the whole world burst into life and color. I've never run a marathon, but I imagine what I felt was something like the post-race euphoria seasoned runners always talk about. I was exhausted, but somehow, I also felt massively energized. It was like an electric current ran through my body: I was done. Done! Within minutes, I'd gone from perpetually stressed and strained to unbelievably free, and I was so giddy I wasn't even quite sure what to do with myself.

But over a celebratory dinner with friends that night, a nagging thought rose like a balloon in my chest. I'd stuffed it down for years. But now that the adrenaline that had fueled me for so long was finally dissipating, it was like someone pumped that balloon up with fresh helium, and it wouldn't stay down. As I pushed my food around my plate, all I could think was: *I just invested three years earning a degree that I don't want to use.*

Confronting this fact made me break out in a cold sweat. My future stretched out in front of me, undefined and shapeless without the comforting framework of semesters to dictate my next steps. I'd only ever been a student with classes to occupy my time and mental energy. For so long, the short-term challenge of exams had distracted me from confronting the bigger questions about my long-term career aspirations. Now that I was poised to enter the workforce, my sudden availability and free time was starting to scare me.

At that celebratory dinner, over talk about job offers and opportunities, that balloon in my chest kept expanding. On the one hand, I envied my friends for their offers, a rarity in a challenging legal job market. But at the same time, I dreaded my own search, because I knew I didn't need to "try on" different legal jobs to confirm that I didn't want to practice law. I'd spent the last three years pretending I didn't know myself quite as well as I actually did. *Who knows*, I thought, *maybe one morning I'll wake up with a burning desire to practice law.* But it was unlikely. At that point, with my legal education finally complete, the mere thought of working as a lawyer was starting to make me feel sick.

And yet, I knew I'd gone to law school for a reason. I loved studying the law, reading about it, discussing it with others, breaking down important issues, doing research: I really, truly enjoyed my legal education. And completing the Bar Exam was an undeniably big deal. I was proud of myself, and I wasn't ready to scrap it all and apply for a job outside the legal profession (at least, not yet). But I could no longer pretend that I had any interest in applying to law firms, working in-house, clerking, or even something tangentially related, like lobbying or policy work. All I could think as I drove home from that celebratory dinner, alone in the dark, was: what the hell am I supposed to do now?

If this story sounds even slightly familiar, you've come to the right place.

Perhaps you're ten years into your legal career and finally taking the time to consider a long overdue career shift. Maybe you've just started to feel pulled in a different direction but you're unsure of your next step. Or maybe you're still in law school, juggling your studies and extracurriculars while constantly quelling the doubts rising in your chest about whether you even want to be a lawyer at all.

Or maybe you're a happy lawyer. You may have been satisfied with your traditional legal career for years or even decades. But now, you might be feeling a bit curious about your friends and colleagues who've forged unique paths. You might be willing to learn more about our expansive, malleable degree and explore the other options that call to you.

No matter where you fall on the spectrum, let me first offer you permission to be curious. While departing from a traditional legal career path can feel daunting or even audacious, it can be resoundingly rewarding.

As lawyers, we're uniquely privileged with options, given the versatility, flexibility, and respectability of our degrees. A "J.D." or "Esquire" after your name gives you gravitas. Even with the proliferation of law schools in different regions and states, the Juris Doctor remains a highly respected degree, and the rigors of law school and legal practice yield themselves to a bevy of transferable skills attractive to employers across industries. And while many practical obstacles (we're looking at you, student loans) may stand in the way of dramatic career shifts, we have far more options than we might think. If we can make it through three years of academic rigor and the pressure of a monstrous exam that holds the keys to our futures, we can surely reinvent ourselves professionally—perhaps even more than once.

I felt pulled to write this book because I've joined the ever-increasing number of lawyers who've pivoted from a traditional legal career path to an unconventional one. But even though I no longer practice law, I still rely heavily on my legal education and experience in my day-to-day work. At no point have I felt that my time spent pursuing a traditional legal career was wasted. I believe that my time spent in law school, studying for the Bar Exam, and practicing law at a private civil litigation firm were all necessary parts of my personal and professional sharpening.

There is a great deal of security and comfort in a traditional legal path. But if we go to law school to expand our minds and open doors, why is it that so many lawyers feel they've limited themselves to one of just a few career tracks?

I've been asked to speak to law students about my experience shifting into a non-traditional legal career. Each time I've done this, I've learned more and more about the common hangups students face when determining how to start their careers. Even those who are certain that they want to explore something unique and non-traditional, perhaps through J.D.-adjacent work, have far more questions than answers:

How did you figure out what you wanted to do?

How do you make money?

Do you ever miss "being a lawyer?"

Do you keep your bar license active?

Do you ever plan to go back to legal practice?

How did you know that your plan was going to work?

What are my options if I don't want to practice?

What if I know I don't want to practice, but I have no clue what I do want?

This book is my attempt to answer those questions.

The Heart Behind This Book

My life was a whirlwind after that celebratory post-Bar dinner. Eleven days later, I got married. My husband, Jacob, and I travelled abroad for two weeks, then when we returned to the States, we moved into a new home. I cried heaving sobs of relief over my Bar letter (that gloriously started with, "We are pleased to inform you"), took the obligatory, "I passed!" picture to send to family and friends, and celebrated. The next day, sitting alone in our newly-settled apartment, I stared at my open laptop with a pit in my stomach. It was time to start looking for a job.

I never wanted to make partner at a law firm. I didn't aspire to become a public defender, an A.U.S.A., a judge. And I never wanted a totalizing career; I knew I desired space to nurture interests and pursuits outside of the law. A 2000-hour billing requirement was incongruous with my goals. Yet I still wanted to work hard, to challenge myself, to be successful, to find a way to use my law degree and legal training in a way that uniquely suited my natural talents while also doing a bit of good. And of course, there was that pesky issue of income: I wanted to contribute to our family's long-term financial well-being. I was determined to land a legal job that satisfied all of these requirements, and application after application, interview after interview, I set out to find one.

I ultimately took a job at a small, well-respected boutique litigation firm just outside of downtown Raleigh. I cut my teeth on personal injury cases and fiduciary disputes, with some business and contract litigation sprinkled in. Because the firm was small, I was handling cases on my own within weeks. This would have been a dream for many young lawyers, but at risk of sounding dramatic, it sucked the very life force out of my bones. The antagonism of the adversarial process gave me tremendous anxiety. The constancy of unforgiving deadlines had me sitting bolt upright in bed at 3 AM and running to check my laptop to confirm I hadn't missed anything. I lived in fear of emails and phone calls, always wondering if something, or someone, was going to pull me into a fight. Though I generally enjoyed public speaking, for some reason, handling motions in court was a different story for me. It made me so nervous that I often become physically ill. This utter lack of confidence and peace was so very unlike me that I started to feel out of place in my own skin.

Though I was paid well and had wonderful colleagues, only 18 months into my career, I was chronically exhausted. My day-to-day work and my innate wiring were severely misaligned. I knew I'd stepped onto a trajectory that was not suitable for the long term. My personal and professional dissonance, and the anxiety it produced, increased the longer I stayed rooted.

After a series of long conversations with Jacob, my parents, close friends, and a few mentors in the legal community who I trusted to keep my personal struggles confidential, I decided it was time for me to move on. I handed in my notice on a bitter cold January day in 2018, with only a vague idea of what I planned to do next: start freelance writing for law firm clients while finding some contract legal work to supplement my income. But more than five years later, I can say that though I initially feared stepping away from a solid, respectable, lucrative career as an attorney, I've found a wealth of opportunities, and robust community, in my non-traditional J.D. career. Though my work still presents unique challenges, the misalignment I felt has dissipated, and I've regained a sense of confidence in my ability to grow and thrive as a professional.

Though our professions are not the core of our identity, our daily work truly does deeply affect every other aspect of our lives. Finding a work situation that does not send us into a constant fight-flight-freeze state is not evidence of the entitlement that millennials are so often castigated for: it is absolutely essential to ensuring that we're positioned to grow in strength, character, and virtue, and to contribute meaningfully to society.

In my current line of work, I've been fortunate to connect with professionals who at one point or another felt similarly misaligned, but found their way into careers that massively energized them. They run companies and non-profits, write books, and host podcasts. They are life coaches for lawyers. They help lawyers buy and sell law practices. They craft and advocate for policies that make the court system more just. They run legal departments. They spearhead diversity and inclusion initiatives within law firms. These creative, dynamic, brilliant individuals teem with energy that animates everything they do. None of them spend valuable time and energy criticizing the legal industry or bellyaching about its faults; they simply found a hole in the market they believed they could serve, and they applied their legal education and training to fill those needs. They, and the profession, are better for it.

None of these individuals followed a preordained path. They pursued work that not only benefitted the profession and employed their skills, but complemented their personalities, interests, and temperaments. Like me, some longed for work that's not quite as frenetic and pressurized as litigation. Others, however, thrived in the fast-paced, high-octane situations that law firm life presents.

I strongly believe one of the keys to professional fulfillment is knowing what type of person you are. Some people are wired for litigation. Some are not. My goal is not to convince you to leave your law firm to teach yoga. You can be just as miserable working 20 hours a week and living a simple life as you are working 60 hours a week in a high-pressure environment. The dissatisfaction stems from misalignment, not the environment itself. To blame the job, the employer, or the profession will only inflame your anxiety and set you up for continued dissatisfaction.

That said, in addition to giving you permission to pivot, this book will also help you figure out the *how* and *why* of your transition. I want to guide you through the internal work necessary to discern who you are, what kind of life suits you, and the type of work that sets you up for long-term success. I want you to know that pivoting is possible as a lawyer, even if you're burdened by student loans. Even if you feel tethered to your identity as a lawyer. Even if you worry about others' expectations or judgments. Even if you can't figure out how to break into another field while still using the degree and the skills you worked so hard to gain.

To give this book more dimension and depth than my personal story ever could, I turned to my community: more than two dozen lawyers who've pivoted into thriving non-traditional J.D. careers. I sat down with each of these professionals to excavate their stories and plumb the depths of their wisdom. All of these individuals graduated from accredited law schools and all but one are licensed to practice law in at least one state. Their careers run the gamut of non-traditional options. And in our hours of interviews, several prevailing, universal themes rose to the surface like oil on water. These themes became the backbone of this book, each standing alone as its own lesson and, ultimately, its own chapter. It was through this collective wisdom that this book was ultimately born.

How This Book is Structured

The three sections of this book are based on what I call the "phases" of career pivoting: discernment, logistics, and mindset. Each section contains short chapters that dive into specific points. Each chapter concludes with a list of reflection questions to help you discern your next career move. I've also included an "action step" that you can take to start to move in the direction of your own pivot. As author Julia Cameron writes in her legendary book *The Artist's Way*: "Whatever you think you can do or believe you can do, begin it. Action has magic, grace, and power in it." [i] That's why I've encouraged you to act, even if that "action" is as seemingly insignificant as sending one email. I highly encourage you to take the time to answer the reflection questions and to complete the action steps. These exercises take this book from a casual read to a tool that can carry you safely and securely through the next few steps of your career transition.

The first section, "Discernment," is about the self-reflection required to identify not only what you want from your career, but also, what type of work best suits your personality, values, professional goals, and skill set. In this section, you'll hear from legal industry entrepreneurs and talented lawyers who work in legal tech, legal operations, and academia.

The second section, "Logistics," is about overcoming the technical obstacles to career changes, from managing student loan debt to networking in a way that doesn't feel sleazy. In this section, you will meet a general counsel-turned-business coach for lawyers; a diversity, equity, and inclusion specialist; the CEO of an international non-profit; and a few other professionals who made dramatic pivots out of a traditional law firm environment and are now thriving personally, professionally, and financially.

The third section, "Mindset," addresses what I've identified as five common mindset challenges that keep many professionals stuck on the same ill-fitting career track. We will round out this section with a few more stories of lawyers who have grappled with one or more of these challenges (and who, occasionally, still do).

Also, because Googling "alternative J.D. careers" can surface a glut of content with varying degrees of credibility, I've compiled a list of resources including websites, books, organizations, and conferences geared toward helping lawyers find their place in an ever-shifting profession.

This book is the product of years of struggling, transitioning, triumphing, struggling again, and eventually, slowly finding my way. It would not exist without the help and support of my family, colleagues, friends, and the legal community at large. If you take nothing else from this book, let it be this: *you don't have to figure this out alone.* In fact, you can't. Lean on your community. Locate your sounding boards. Identify your mentors. And when all is said and done, give it back. Return, or pass on, the generosity that others have shown you as you stumbled around on baby deer legs, trying to find your way in an intimidating legal landscape.

In my own career, countless people have carried me. This is my attempt to offer the same support to others.

SECTION 1

Discernment

"If it scares you, it might be a good thing to try."

—Seth Godin

CHAPTER 1
Ignite Your Pilot Light

"The best way to figure out what you want is to
start doing things and see what lands."

When I talk to law students who don't want to practice law, they
often ask: *how did you figure out what you actually wanted to do?* I
almost always laugh and ask them how much time they have. The
truth is, I have no idea. And frankly, I still am not entirely sure what
I "want to do" long-term.

Sometimes, the internal work required to discern our professional
interests can be even more difficult than managing the logistical
challenges involved in a seismic career shift. And though this
internal work is incredibly important, many young professionals get
stuck on this initial step. They focus far too much on figuring out
the "what" that they fail to just take the first step, and so, like me,
they wind up in a traditional legal job that they don't like for much
longer than they should.

When we fixate on finding the single "right thing," we paralyze ourselves. Too much emphasis on discernment and inner work can prevent us from actually acting. Reflection and internal work are vital, but they are just small pieces of the greater picture. They should never stand alone, but always, *always* be coupled with intentional, prudent action: micro steps in a direction, any direction, to gain some clarity on where we should turn next in our professional lives.

In my meetings with other non-traditional lawyers, a common theme swirled to the surface of my scattered interview notes: try as we might to deny it, we all have *some* internal motivation, something we love to do, something we feel we are *made* to do. And while many (possibly, most) people will not end up making a career out of it, many will. Those who don't make a career out of it will nonetheless incorporate it into their lives in some way. Regardless of whether it ever generates income, identifying this internal motivation can bring purpose, energy, and clarity to our professional lives. If we deny it, we might continue to feel misaligned in our work, and possibly even in our lives outside of work.

Attorney, author, entrepreneur, and coach Davina Frederick calls this internal motivation a "pilot light:" a tiny flicker that may be dormant, but when stoked, can erupt into brilliant, illuminating flames. We will meet Davina shortly, but first, I'd like to share a bit of my backstory and how I've wrestled with this "pilot light" concept in my own career.

From Lawyer to Professional Writer

Like many lawyers, I've always loved stories. The first time someone asked me what I wanted to be when I grew up, I was seven, and I was at the dentist's office. "A writer," I blurted through bubble-gum toothpaste. But as I progressed through high school and into college, like many, I assumed that "being a writer" was synonymous with "being broke," so I dismissed the possibility of pursuing a degree in creative writing. I majored in English so I could circle around others who, too, wanted to make it in a creative career, then marched headlong into law school, hoping to find even more kindred spirits there.

I was disappointed and more than just a little disillusioned to learn that law school is not exactly a Mecca for creative types, but I did find it incredibly intellectually sharpening. And in between learning the Rules of Evidence and practicing my moot court arguments, I never stopped writing. I blogged. I joined *Law Review* and wrote about international law. In my (scant) downtime, I wrote short stories and personal essays about the unique characters I met in law school. And even when graduation approached and I started to feel increasingly gloomy about my career choice and my inevitable job hunt, I convinced myself that I would always, always be a writer, no matter what I did from 9-5 on Monday through Friday.

When I found out I passed the North Carolina Bar Exam, I applied to civil litigation law firms, as one does, because people told me that litigators do a lot of writing. Combine frustrated expectations with my temperament—which is decidedly *not* suited to the adversarial nature of litigation—and you've got a recipe for misery.

I liked my employers and appreciated how generously they invested in my career. They helped me identify practice areas I liked more than others, taught me how to navigate difficult relationships with opposing counsel, and sat in the courtroom with me while I fumbled my way through my first few motions. I knew that *they* weren't the problem. Moving to another firm wouldn't help. The *work itself* was an ill-fitting garment.

Even though I knew I needed to step away from my litigation career, I never thought that I could make a living as a writer. I'm no Ann Patchett, so quitting my legal job to write a memoir wasn't an option. But the writing life still pulled on my sleeves. And something kept telling me that the cure for my misalignment wouldn't be found in a litigation career, or even a more research and writing-heavy legal role like clerking.

Complicating matters further, I knew I'd gone to law school for a reason. I felt drawn to the law. I wasn't ready to abandon it. But I wasn't sure what was next for me. I was only 28 years old and already feeling terribly stuck, lost, and a little bit hopeless.

That Pesky Little Thing Called Money

When I finally decided it was time to leave my law firm, a practical hurdle stopped me in my tracks: *finances*. Though my husband was an attorney as well, like most other couples, we needed both of our incomes. Quitting my job without a solid plan on how to replace my income simply wasn't an option for us. If I wanted to quit, I needed to find a job with a commensurate salary, or, at least, something close to it, as quickly as possible.

One day in April of 2017, when a small town North Carolina jury deliberated on the securities fraud case our firm had been trying for the past week, I pulled a flattened peanut butter sandwich out of my purse and started Googling "how to make money as a writer" on my iPhone. I'm not entirely sure what possessed me to start researching this topic that particular moment: maybe it was my sheer delirious exhaustion from weeks of preparing for trial. But it was enormously fruitful. I stumbled upon article after article, website after website, touting the benefits of a freelance writing career. I learned that writers can not only earn money for their work, but they can do quite well. In some cases, they can even make six-figures. Specifically, highly specialized freelance writing niches, like legal or medical, could yield a healthy income, particularly for those who cut their teeth ghostwriting for high-profile firms or industry leaders.

I think I could do this, I thought, taking a bite of my stale sandwich. *I can be a writer. I can work for lawyers. Lawyers can be my clients.* It seemed like the perfect marriage of my two loves: language and the law.

As appealing as this path sounded, at this point, l had no clue how to make this type of work an income-generating reality. How would I find clients? How would I convince lawyers that I could ghostwrite for them? Could I replace my law firm salary? Would people think I'd failed at legal practice and was trying to prop up my dying career? Was this a really dumb idea? These questions, and many others, looped around my brain for the next few months.

I didn't have answers to any of these questions, but I had a feeling I could figure it out. And I was ready to try.

I launched my ghostwriting business, Davis Legal Media, in April 2018, exactly one year after that day in the courthouse gallery. Though it took a full year, I did eventually replace my law firm salary. Eighteen months later, I nearly doubled it.

"I See You're a Lawyer."
Something clicked when I told myself it was okay to pursue work I enjoyed. Not only did my increased career satisfaction infuse new energy into my marriage, friendships, and family life, but I realized that my legal background and experience impacted my writing career in ways I'd never anticipated.

The publications and organizations I pitched for writing and speaking opportunities viewed my law degree as an asset even though I was not practicing. Opportunities to write, speak, teach, or serve on boards have stemmed from someone noting, *I see you're a lawyer.* Even when I respond, *right, but I'm not practicing law right now*, they invariably say something like, *I know. I don't care.* People seem to trust lawyers naturally and instinctively. The pressure cooker of law school, Bar prep, and the realities of legal practice shape us into sharp, thoughtful professionals poised to make valuable contributions to the marketplace of ideas. For this reason, I've kept my license active, even though I'm not currently using it.

From Burned-Out Solo Practitioner to Wealthy Woman Lawyer
Attorney, author, coach, entrepreneur, and popular podcaster Davina

Frederick started law school at age 38 after a long and successful career in marketing. When she felt the pull to shift gears from the field in which she'd developed so much expertise, she narrowed her choices to teaching, psychology, and law. Her cousin convinced her to choose law, but she always knew, in the back of her mind, that entrepreneurship called to her. And it always would.

When she graduated from law school in 2007, Davina started her own law firm in the midst of the foreclosure crisis in her home state of Florida. She served as local counsel for lenders in foreclosure cases and after a few successes led to a steady stream of revenue, she brought in a partner. The foreclosure cases were their bread and butter, a reliable source of income while they each cultivated their practice areas of interest: for Davina, divorce, estate planning, and business, and for her partner, real estate.

But despite her success, a few years in, Davina started to feel the nag of dissatisfaction and the imminence of burnout. The plight common to the solo practitioner had struck. She was doing it *all*. She was simultaneously the Managing Partner, Firm Administrator, and Unofficial Therapist to her clients and team.

"It was constant pressure," she told me. "It wasn't my clients who were the issue. It was opposing counsel." The antagonism unique to the adversarial process left Davina feeling constantly stressed, like she was "in for a fight every day." And while she was more than capable of handling it, Davina said, "it wasn't who I was. I didn't want that lifestyle." On top of the constant antagonism was the mess of frustrated expectations common to overwhelmed attorneys: "We fall in love with the glamour of being an attorney," she explained, "and then we get into the day-to-day of it, and it's not what we expected."

This stress and relentless pressure negatively impacted Davina's health. She gained weight and struggled with depression. It was evident that she needed a dramatic change, and soon. Though she wasn't sure what her next move would be, Davina started by taking one step. She struck a deal with her partner, who bought her out of the practice. This gave her the time and space to discern her next steps.

At the same time, Davina and her husband owned a CrossFit gym in central Florida, and after she left her practice, Davina started working in the gym, helping to run its daily operations. Filling her newfound free time at the gym had its perks. Davina started to exercise regularly. She lost weight and started to regain some of the energy her law practice had siphoned. With this renewed energy and strength, so, too, came her resolve to find her next professional contribution.

This gradual process of restoring her health, energy, and mental clarity led Davina to open another law firm, this time, a virtual estate planning practice. It was 2011, and the virtual realm, though burgeoning, was not nearly what it is today. Naysayers emerged from the woodwork to tell Davina about the many ways this model was bound to fail. But her clients loved it, especially her homebound, elderly estate planning clients, who were understandably happy to handle their legal affairs without getting into a car.

This role agreed with Davina much more than her previous practice did, but she still felt something was lacking. "I was doing it because I'd become a lawyer and I invested all this time and money, but it still wasn't catching my soul on fire," she said.

So, when an attorney friend invited Davina to attend a coaching conference with her, Davina agreed, curious about what she might learn. The event was full of pump-up music, flashing lights, and tearfully gushing testimonials about the life-changing power of coaching, but Davina's first one-on-one coaching experience left her admittedly confused about the hype. It was her second coach, though, who ignited a spark that then turned into a steady, burning flame. "She completely changed everything for me," Davina said, "because we did a lot of mindset work." Her coach helped her peel back the layers hiding the beating heart beneath her professional dissatisfaction. This undeniably positive coaching experience lit a fire under Davina to start helping others find similar clarity in their careers and lives. Though she didn't necessarily know it at the time, this was Davina's pilot light, and it was now steadily burning.

Throughout the following months, Davina started talking to other women lawyers who were intensely struggling to run profitable law firms while staying sane, organized, healthy, and financially solvent. These conversations were illuminating: Davina started to realize that while women lawyers knew how to serve clients, they didn't know how to build and run profitable businesses. After years of running her own practices and figuring out how to create a financially solvent law firm business, Davina felt a clarion call to share what she had learned.

With this new energy and clarity, Davina officially started taking on coaching clients. She started by helping entrepreneurs run more efficient, profitable businesses, but eventually, she refined her focus and narrowed her niche. She now helps women law firm owners create wealth-generating law firms without sacrificing their well-being in the process. Her company, Wealthy Woman Lawyer, has expanded into multiple group and individual coaching programs and a popular podcast. She has helped hundreds of women scale their law firms while building a team and creating systems and processes to keep their practices running even while they rest.

Davina went from representing lenders in foreclosures to running a CrossFit gym, to growing a virtual law practice, to coaching. She went from burned-out lawyer to entrepreneur and educator with a healthy personal life and a company whose mission aligns with her personal values. But safe to say, *run a company that helps women scale their law firms* probably wasn't what she told people at cocktail parties who asked her what she wanted to do. Her career developed step by small, seemingly inconsequential step.

Taking a break from practicing.

Attending a coaching conference.

Finding another coach after she didn't connect with her first one.

Hanging her shingle as a coach and growing her skills.

Niching down.

Constantly re-evaluating her priorities, goals, and strengths alongside the market's needs.

"It was definitely an evolution," Davina told me. "The best way to figure out what you want is to start doing things and see what lands."

Before she launched her coaching career, Davina felt hampered by well-meaning but often unsolicited advice from her friends and colleagues. Wise counsel is essential, but when you consume too many opinions, it can be nearly impossible to locate your pilot light. External factors like others' expectations, and certainly stress and burnout, operate like a fire blanket: they snuff out any spark that threatens to break through. Consuming too much external content, opinions, or advice can confuse us, especially when we're on the precipice of a significant career shift. The antidote is clear-headed, intentional, prudent action, step by small step.

For Davina, as for many others, one-on-one coaching was an instrumental tool in finding clarity on her next steps. It lit her pilot light and allowed her to think clearly about what interests and passions were tugging on her own heart, instead of exposing her inner struggle to the court of public opinion.

On Childhood Passions and Departing from the Mainstream
James Porter works as a Director of Contracts in the legal tech space. He drafts, negotiates, and manages contracts for his organization, using his legal education and business skills to craft innovative solutions to streamline the contract life cycle. Unlike most of his law school classmates, James didn't take the Bar Exam

or apply for clerkships. After graduating from law school, he immediately started to work in the legal tech space.

When I asked James for his advice for law students who aren't married to the prospect of a traditional legal role, he encouraged intense self-reflection: not only after graduating, but throughout law school as well. Law school courses and extracurricular opportunities can lend valuable insight into our unique interests and strengths.

This self-reflection led James away from activities like moot court or *Law Review* and toward social opportunities like running for a leadership position within the Student Bar Association. "I thought this would separate me and allow for more opportunities," he explained. He also shared that in law school, the push to achieve coveted spots in activities like *Law Review* and mock trial can lead students to spend massive amounts of time on activities that are not only misaligned with their own interests and desires, but also, set them on the wrong trajectory. "I didn't ever want to create an environment where I didn't have options because I spent three years trying to be like everyone else," he told me.

Law school culture can make it challenging to connect with those innate desires. I asked James about how to get in touch with what really motivates and excites us when the environment around us pushes a few idealized activities or paths. His advice: take time to reflect on the activities, causes, or pursuits that caught your attention when you were younger, before external opinions clouded your vision.

"Who were you, and what did you want to be? What separates

you from other people? Try to choose things that are somewhat connected with that," James said. For him, it wasn't so much a particular cause, field, or professional identity, but an undeniable fact about himself: he is a social person who draws energy from others. This self-knowledge was tremendous for James because it eliminated a massive swath of possible career paths that involve intense periods of individualized work, like research and writing (i.e., an awful lot of traditional legal careers).

Yet there is hope for people who take a path only to find out years later that they are deeply misaligned and out of touch with who they are or what they want. Enduring the rigors of law school and becoming a lawyer can be a tremendous asset to your long-term career, even if you end up using your degree in a non-traditional way. As James shared: "It will enhance your marketability regardless of the industry or type of work you eventually pursue."

Jealousy is a Map

One powerful way to locate our pilot lights, our internal motivations, our values, is to pay attention to what makes us feel envious. We're all primed to eschew jealousy as a "green monster," a virus and a vice. And in many contexts, it is. But it can also be a valuable tool.

Once again, I quote Julia Cameron from *The Artist's Way*: "Jealousy is a map." It can lend insight into the types of jobs and lives that attract us.

When I was practicing law, I felt intensely envious of my friends with flexible schedules and the freedom to set their own priorities. All of these people were self-employed. I did *not* feel envious of my friends who worked in Big Law or who achieved great success in the corporate world. I felt more envious of those with simpler, less glamorous lives, even those who made less money than I did.

At first, I berated myself for letting envy take root in my soul. But I also knew that it was something I shouldn't dismiss. Throughout my life, there was a common thread throughout every person or situation that sparked envy in my heart. I started to let myself get a bit curious about this envy. Why was I envious of the same types of people, again and again? Why was I so attracted to a certain kind of lifestyle? Why did I consistently choose to follow paths that looked different than all of the ones I admired? Could I, too, pursue a life that felt appealing, sustainable, inspiring, and even enjoyable?

It's helpful to pay attention to your envy instead of dismissing it. Resist the urge to chastise yourself for feeling it, and instead, ask yourself *why* you feel that way and *what*, specifically, about a particular person or situation makes you feel envious. The answer might give you more honest, accurate data than any other form of self-reflection. And frankly, unless you're jealous of Beyonce because you, too, want her money and fame, the particular thing you envy probably is much more attainable than you think.

Reflection Questions

Think back to your pre-law school days. How would you describe yourself? What did you do for fun? What topics sparked your curiosity? Who did you spend time with?

If money were no object, what would you spend your days doing? (Keep in mind that "drinking beer on the beach" would get old, so push yourself to think a little more deeply. What would you *actually* love doing if you didn't need to earn a paycheck? What would get you out of bed if the pressure to pay bills no longer existed?)

Do you volunteer for any organizations or donate to any causes? Why do you spend your time and/or money on them? Our financial habits, and how we spend our free time, lend insight into what we value.

Is there anyone in your immediate circle whose job piques your interest? What is it about their career that intrigues you?

What (or rather, who) makes you envious and why?

Action Step
Take an hour or two to answer these questions as honestly as possible. Don't critique yourself as you answer them or respond the way you think you "should." You will revisit your answers later.

CHAPTER 2
Look Up the Ladder

"If you dread reaching the top rung of the ladder you're climbing, stop climbing and start figuring out which ladders around you make you want to be the first to the top."

Many new law school graduates are just grateful to land a job. Any job. After all, a job means experience, entry into the market, and a paycheck: all very valuable things, especially in a challenging economy. But it's worth taking a slightly longer view of your career and asking yourself where you are bound to end up if you succeed in your current role. In other words, to whom do you report? Is theirs the job you'll eventually have? Do you know anything about the position and its day-to-day responsibilities? Is this a job that you'd want? Is this a *life* that you'd want? Are you happy with the direction you're heading, or do you need to pivot now before you get too deeply entrenched, too comfortable, too settled?

Nearly every lawyer I know who's left a traditional legal career told me that this thought experiment—this glance up the ladder—

catalyzed their pivots. This is not a slight against the people running their organizations; it actually has nothing at all to do with those people. It does, however, have a great deal to do with you, the person considering a career pivot. If you're growing in your career but you dread reaching the top rung of the ladder you're climbing, stop climbing and start figuring out which ladders around you make you want to be the first to the top.

Continuing this thought experiment, it's vital to learn a bit about your superior's life *outside of* the office as well. Is this person happy? A Big Law lawyer I know shared this advice: find out whether the partners to whom you report protect their time outside the office. Are they sending you emails at midnight on a Sunday? Do they ever take vacations? Are they out of touch when they're out of town?

It is short-sighted *not* to consider what your specific job responsibilities will be if you remain in your current firm, company, or organization long enough to advance. And while there is certainly room to pivot ten, fifteen, or even twenty years into your career, consider the opportunity cost of sticking around instead of switching gears early on, before you grow comfortable with your role, your salary, and the benefits of working for your particular organization.

Reflection Questions

What are you working toward? Whose position will you ultimately take if you advance in your current firm, company, or organization?

Who is one step above you in your organization? What about two or three steps? What do their daily tasks and responsibilities look like?

Do you like these people? Do you respect them? Do they appear satisfied with their work? Are they happy? Would you want their jobs? Their lives?

Action Step

It's time to gather data. Identify a colleague who's a few years ahead of you or a few levels of seniority above you in your organization. Take this person to coffee and ask about their day-to-day work. Get a sense of what it would be like to advance in your organization. Ask specific questions about what their day-to-day tasks involve, not just big picture, overarching themes about what they do and who they serve.

Then, take stock of the people you know who've left your organization before being promoted. What did they do after they left? Do you see any patterns in what the departing employees are now doing for work? Can you find out why they left? What is their new role giving them that the previous one didn't? What specific skills and experiences did they take with them, and how are these skills and experiences benefiting them now?

If you're a law student, here's a variation of this exercise:

Ask your law school career services office to point you to three or four alumni who are about 15-20 years into their careers. Ideally, try to identify people across practice areas or industries, e.g., private sector, public sector, in-house, etc. Ask each person if you can schedule an informational interview via Zoom to learn a bit about their careers.

The key to gleaning valuable insight from an informational interview is asking questions that are as narrow and specific as possible. Here are a few examples:

Instead of: What's a typical day like?
Ask: What are three projects are you working on right now?

Instead of: What do you like about your job?
Ask: what was most exciting to you this week? And what is one thing you wish was different about your situation?

Instead of: What advice do you have for me?
Ask: What is one thing I can do right now to prepare myself for a job like yours?

Instead of: Do you have work-life balance?
Ask: Is there a billing requirement? If so, how many hours? Approximately how many hours do you work per week?

Other questions that can be incredibly illuminating are:

- What's your office culture like?

- What was your most stressful day or moment in the office, and why?

- What attributes would make someone a bad fit for this role?

- Would you ever consider leaving? Why?

- What would keep you there? or what makes you stay?

- What keeps you up at night?

- Who is the best hire you've made recently, and why?

CHAPTER 3
Inventory Your Skills

"You have to break out of that mindset of, 'I don't know how to do anything except write a motion'."

One of the greatest disappointments in our profession is the sheer number of smart, capable lawyers who think they can't do anything except draft motions and write briefs. Even if our work experience is limited to a more traditional legal role, the truth is we can extrapolate, rebrand, or reframe any task to fit a much broader context. This can persuade a prospective employer that you are capable of handling the job responsibilities, even if your background looks dramatically different than the role you are seeking.

A few examples of a tasks reframe are:

Drafting motions = *Persuasive writing*.

Arguing with adjusters = *Negotiation*.

Client counselling / case strategy = *Risk management.*

Case law research= *Data analysis.*

Trying cases = *Public speaking.*

Developing case strategy = *Project management.*

When I first started my business, I felt completely lost. I had never run a business before, I had no marketing or sales experience, I had no idea how to build a website, and terms like ROI and KPIs were utterly foreign to me. I didn't know what entity type I should choose when registering the business, how to file my taxes, or how to hire contractors or employees (and which option would be better for my business).

But in legal practice, I'd helped clients form their own entities. *I could figure out which type was best for me.*

I developed a sense of financial savvy as an associate poring over reams of client financial records in the discovery process. *If I could decipher these, I could surely figure out how to file my taxes.*

At the firm, I watched my employers grow their own thriving business and connect authentically with their clients, colleagues, and referral sources. *I didn't have to learn "sales." I had to connect meaningfully with people I wanted to work with.*

Upon reflection, I began to realize that my two years as an

associate at a small law firm—a small *business*—prepared me for entrepreneurship in ways I never could have imagined. Most importantly, my employers and my role helped me develop a certain grit and "I can figure this out" attitude unique to lawyers (and small firm lawyers in particular). This mentality has helped me push through various challenges in my nearly six years of running and growing a small business. Not to mention, after navigating the stress of litigation, the minor challenges that popped up from time to time in my small business paled in comparison. My time in legal practice thickened my skin. Small challenges didn't incapacitate me quite as much. I'd survived challenging projects and clients before, and I forged ahead with the confidence that I could do so again.

From Big Law to Wellness Coaching for Lawyers

Matt Hrutkay spent ten years in Big Law before realizing he was severely misaligned. "I just started asking myself *why*," he said. "Why was I driving myself crazy? Why was I checking my email at ten o'clock at night? Why was that okay?"

Matt's Big Law salary afforded many privileges, like a generous budget for international travel. Yet even when he took time off to travel, the vacations were not especially refreshing: the pressure to check his email and remain on-call never abated. Added to the constant pressure of his job was the urgency to fully relish his time away before returning to the grind. All of these external and internal pressures made Matt realize something vital about rest and the human condition. "You can't just cram rest into a single ten-day period," he said.

Matt longed to design a life in which he didn't have to fight so hard for rest, where relaxation looked less like a boxer grabbing a quick swig of water and wiping the blood from his face before jumping back into the ring. And after a while, it became clear to Matt that giving up Big Law prestige for entrepreneurship was a critical first step. To gain more freedom, he would also have to let go of the generous pay and undeniable prestige of his Big Law job, but the toll on his mental and physical health had simply become too much. After a decade climbing the Big Law ladder, Matt offered his resignation.

Matt's unlikely portal into entrepreneurship was his motorcycle, which he purchased shortly after leaving his Big Law career in hopes that a new hobby would restore a sense of delight in his day-to-day life. As he wound through the picturesque West Coast routes he commuted day after day, something became abundantly evident to him: *he wanted more of that*. More of that release. That freedom. That spirit of adventure. That wholehearted living he left Big Law to find. "I realized how much I missed fun!" Matt told me. Believing he could find that kind of freedom, release, and wholeheartedness by designing his own work-play rhythms, Matt launched his own law firm and started picking up clients and cases in his small California town.

A few years into running his solo practice, Matt realized that the substantial reduction in his baseline stress level freed up his mental and emotional resources. With this new bandwidth, he was ready to take the time to figure out what was next for him. It so happened that he'd been feeling increasingly pulled to the well-being and mental health space. He had done a tremendous amount of work to heal through his own mental health challenges and started to see an increasing number of lawyers speak openly about theirs. After connecting with other lawyers who were working through pandemic-related burnout and other mental health issues, Matt enrolled in a coaching training program to see if he could find a way to help these lawyers recover. He knew that a coaching certification would position him to help more people than he could by simply sharing his personal story.

In the Summer of 2021, Matt officially started to introduce himself publicly as a wellness coach for lawyers and began a slow and gradual transition out of full-time legal practice. His coaching business caught fire: more and more lawyers started approaching him for one-on-one coaching, and his work eventually burgeoned into a full-time coaching business with a healthy client roster. Matt now spends his days helping lawyers find peace and purpose in their practices while maintaining their physical and mental health. Coaching is now this former Big Law attorney's full time gig, and Matt couldn't be happier about it.

At its heart, Matt's pivot was about recognizing the malleability of his skill set—years of hard and soft skills that could contribute to a broad swath of services, industries, and opportunities. Recognizing this, however, required a reframe. "You have to break out of that mindset of, *I don't know how to do anything except write a motion,*" he said. "There are partners at top law firms who think they don't have options."

The key, Matt told me, is learning to translate your legal work experience into a non-legal language to convince a hiring committee, investors, or potential customers that you know what you're doing. "Say, *I've managed projects. I've formed companies.* You can connect your existing skills to the context you want to be in."

Taking an Old Service to a New Context

Tom Lenfestey helps lawyers buy and sell law practices through his company, Law Practice Exchange, a business that he calls "the marriage of a passion project and entrepreneurship."

Before he launched his company, Tom's legal practice experience was transactional: tax, business, and estate planning. What interested him most about his transactional work wasn't necessarily the legal work itself; it was watching the professionals he was guiding hire brokers to sell or exit their companies.

After watching countless entrepreneurs build up value in their businesses and sell them for a healthy profit, Tom realized that he didn't have a succession plan for his own law firm. But when he set out to create one, he was forced to look to other industries for examples of how to do it. He could find no information specifically speaking to the sale or dissolution of a law practice. Tom started to wonder who, if anyone, was helping lawyers manage those legally precarious transactions. He searched his network and learned that there was, indeed, a gaping hole in the legal marketplace for such services.

Law Practice Exchange was born from this scarcity, starting as an educational hub for lawyers seeking to create succession plans for their practices. Tom first tested his idea by pitching it to the North Carolina Bar Association and Lawyers' Mutual, two organizations with which he was already connected through his legal practice. "I knew that if they laughed me out of the building then it wasn't such a great idea," he said. "But both organizations received it with open arms because they were getting a lot of calls from attorneys who didn't have a succession plan."

Tom's next step, then, was to launch a program that taught attorneys how to buy and sell a law practice. "I didn't know if we'd even get five lawyers there," he said, "but we maxed out. And we did that program on repeat."

As he gained notoriety as an expert in *creating* law firm succession plans, Tom eventually started to take on clients who wanted him to *execute* their plans. He responded to this demand by shifting from educational programming to creating and managing succession plans for real law firms, helping lawyers retire from their practices while keeping the firms intact and preserving their value for a future generation of lawyers.

For aspiring entrepreneurs pursuing a business concept that's new and untested, Tom recommends taking any opportunity to talk to your prospective client base. "Get out there and say, *look, you may not have thought about this before. It may be an option for you.*" Tom told me that growing such a business might require fighting your legal wiring. "In law school, we're trained to look at a set of facts and find the absolute worst-case scenario. And that's what lawyers do in practice," he said. "And so, we are trained to think first why something won't work, instead of thinking why it *will*."

When he first developed the idea for Law Practice Exchange, Tom continued to run his law firm, with no immediate plans to shut it down. He kept his practice active as a backup, which allowed him to grow his business slowly and without intense pressure to immediately replace his revenue. This is what allowed Law Practice Exchange to develop the strong roots necessary for steady, consistent, and eventually, massive growth.

Tom's clients have themselves proven the value of the slow, intentional, gradual transition. Many of his clients pursue other careers upon exiting their firms. Some break into real estate or other business ventures, and many of them do quite well because the day-to-day of running a law firm builds a certain grit and savvy that translates into other business contexts. But Tom explained that the most successful of his clients are the ones who (1) don't take a leap on a whim, but rather, their transition is born from years (or even decades) of preparation; and (2) see, and capitalize upon, a gap in the market.

Tom has applied these principles throughout his own entrepreneurial path. Law Practice Exchange is not a novel concept. He simply identified an existing business model that worked well in other industries, and brought it to the legal field. Now, his company serves clients throughout the U.S. and Canada.

Reflection Questions

What practical, legal, or "soft" skills have you honed in your current position?

What type of feedback is your employer giving you? Your colleagues? Your clients? Are there patterns or common threads in your performance evaluations?

Have you had any tangible triumphs, breakthroughs, or successes in your career thus far? What are they?

Action Step

Try this Resume Reframe exercise:

- Write down all of your current job responsibilities, anything you've ever achieved, or any project (or case) you've handled. Don't forget to include items that are not strictly legal, like helping your firm roll out a new marketing campaign, spearheading a pro bono project, writing articles, or teaching CLEs.

- Isolate each item and rename it so it applies to a general vs. a strictly legal context. For example, "client counselling" can become "expectation management" and "handling mediations" can be "negotiation."

- Identify a few roles or industries that pique your interest. Read the job descriptions.

- For each one, rewrite your resume, retooling your specific skills and experiences to be responsive to the job description.

Take your rewritten resume(s) to a trusted colleague or mentor for feedback (keep in mind that your current employers may not be the best choice if your desired career change is news to them).

If you aren't sure where to start, try the career development office at your law school. Most of the time, the staff are more than willing to help graduates navigate career transitions, and they'll likely have data to share about other graduates who've explored non-traditional J.D. careers. Better yet, they may even have a bank of resumes and cover letters to give you a sense of how to structure your own materials.

CHAPTER 4
Raise Your Hand

*"At the end of the day, who better than
you to do something?"*

When you're presented with a new opportunity in your
organization or firm, resist the urge to turn it down because you're
already overwhelmed or you are certain you don't have the time. This
seemingly arbitrary new opportunity may inspire your pivot.

To illustrate, I want to share the career story of my law school
classmate Jeff Cox, the Director of Content for UniCourt, a legal
tech company that provides real-time access to court data and legal
analytics powered by an API-first platform.

"Who Better Than You?"

Jeff paved his path to UniCourt through relentless curiosity and
an openness to new opportunities. When he graduated from law
school, Jeff's goal was to land an in-house counsel position. But

like many new lawyers, he felt stymied by the maddening advice to *get some experience first*. Of course, this advice only generates *more* questions, like, *how am I supposed to get experience when everyone wants to hire people who already have it?*

For Jeff, the answer was motion. He needed to land a job quickly and didn't have time to agonize, so he started applying to legal industry roles that looked even slightly interesting. He ultimately applied for a legal operations role with Citigroup, and was invited to an interview. In law school, Jeff conducted a 50-state survey on employment discrimination filings. He brought the results of his research to the interview as tangible proof of his analytical skills and ability to handle massive research projects. It worked: Citigroup offered Jeff a job as a legal operations analyst, and though it wasn't exactly what he'd wanted, Jeff accepted the position.

Jeff's work for Citigroup bore fruit he never could have expected. A few months in, a managing director for the legal operations team resigned, and Jeff volunteered to help take on the role of Global Conflict Relationship Manager for Citigroup. "This was quite possibly the best thing I ever did," Jeff told me. "Often, when you raise your hand to volunteer for certain things, you get really good hands-on experience."

As a new attorney, Jeff was managing conflicts of interest for Citigroup globally, speaking with the managing partners of Am Law firms worldwide and interfacing with every quadrant of the company's legal and business teams. This culminated in a few more pivots, including becoming an Assistant VP of Outside Counsel

Management, which enabled Jeff to work on rewriting Citigroup's legal policy (also something to which he volunteered) and co-creating a corporate legal pro bono committee locally in Tampa, Florida.

But even as he ascended to increasingly higher levels of seniority within Citigroup, Jeff sensed a gap between his current role (dynamic as it was) and the type of intellectual, creative challenges he craved: he wanted to write and publish on topics of interest, specifically, how artificial intelligence (AI) was changing legal services. He contacted the Association of Corporate Counsel (ACC) and asked to write an article about AI and the law. They agreed and asked him to interview three legal tech companies who were using AI.

Josh Blandi, the CEO of UniCourt, was one of the three CEOs Jeff interviewed. What was intended to be a 30-minute interview with Josh lasted for two and a half hours. Jeff took the reams of information from the interview to his writing process, which was a success. The ACC published the article, and shortly after it went live, Josh contacted Jeff to offer him a part-time position ghostwriting articles for UniCourt's blog and external by-lined articles.

It took Jeff several months to gain Citigroup's approval to take on a side job. But when they did, Jeff started regularly ghostwriting articles about AI, data, and access to justice for major industry publications like the *American Bar Association*, *Above the Law*, and *Legaltech News*.

After several months of ghostwriting while working for Citigroup,

Jeff was offered a full-time role as UniCourt's Director of Content. He gladly accepted, even though the role was a departure from his initial plan to go in-house. Had he remained fixated on his original plan, Jeff would not have explored ghostwriting, he never would have met Josh, and he would not have written his own ticket to a successful career in a sector that is constantly growing.

Pivoting to full-time work with UniCourt benefited Jeff personally and financially. But it also gave him the time and freedom to dive headlong into legal aid work, which Jeff calls his "true calling." Specifically, leaving the corporate world gave him the flexibility to serve on the Board of Directors of Bay Area Legal Services, one of the largest non-profit law firms in the State of Florida. The team at UniCourt encouraged Jeff's volunteerism, viewing it as an asset rather than a distraction, and Jeff's service to Bay Area Legal Services opened opportunities he never could have anticipated. Recently, he has been invited to chair the Veterans Committee to raise funds for legal services for veterans, and he was selected to serve as the Secretary of the Board. As Jeff says, "this can all be summed up with one of my favorite sayings: 'The reward for good work is more work.'"

Jeff's career path proves how one small yes after another, as well as a service-oriented heart, can lead to organic, self-perpetuating career developments. Sometimes, these small yeses can morph into something much larger than the sum of each individual response.

In law school, we're trained to stand up and make arguments under pressure, recite the facts of cases, manage enormous swaths of information, then sit for an exam that dictates the future of our careers. If anyone is accustomed to pressure, it's lawyers. Simply shooting an email to someone you want to learn from, or asking for an opportunity, or saying yes to a new challenge, pales in comparison.

As Jeff says, "Just go do it. You've been trained well. At the end of the day, who better than you to do something?"

The Value of Pro Bono Work

In addition to saying yes to new opportunities, consider the value of pro bono work to your long-term career, particularly if you are looking to pivot. Taking on a pro bono project requires a tremendous step outside of your comfort zone. Not only does it demand learning the mechanics of a potentially unfamiliar area of law, but it can also involve working alongside lawyers and clients from a range of backgrounds. This type of departure from the tried-and-true can foster the confidence required to make a career pivot.

Pro bono work also provides an outlet for honing the "soft skills" necessary to pivot, like networking, relationship-building, and developing creative solutions to new problems. Within local bar associations, lawyers committed to giving their time and talent to pro bono work is legion. Take advantage of every opportunity to meet these service-minded lawyers, whether through happy hours, CLEs, or networking events. They could be your future co-workers.

Reflection Questions

What opportunities at work, whether new projects or clients, pro bono work, or other opportunities, have you said "yes" to lately?

Looking back, can you see what new skill sets or experiences those opportunities have yielded?

Is your natural tendency to say yes to new opportunities or to defer or delay them? If the latter, how do you think you can train yourself to be receptive to new opportunities, even the ones that do not seem immediately fruitful?

How can you create time in your schedule for additional commitments? Are there other, lower-value activities you can defer for a while, or any tasks you can outsource?

Action Step

Identify someone outside your organization whose career intrigues you. Reach out to that person and invite them to coffee (even just virtual coffee: send them coffee money via Venmo and set up a Zoom meeting.). Interview them about their work, life, and career path. As they share, pay special attention to the small steps, the yeses, that opened doors for them.

Then, devise a plan to start saying yes more often in your own organization or career. Commit to becoming more observant of the opportunities that flow from seemingly small commitments and connections.

For example, at the start of each week, set an intention to say yes to something small. Write it down as a promise to yourself. For instance, you could write: *This week, I will say yes to volunteering at the expunction clinic or I will say yes when asked if I can stay late to discuss a new case.*

A Few Practical Ideas:

- In your local community or bar association, there are likely a number of organizations, clubs, civic groups, or meet-ups that will surround you with the type of work you are interested in, or at least people that do that type of work. Choose one to explore.

- If there are opportunities in your firm or organization that look appealing, perhaps a new practice area niche, step up to volunteer your time.

- Better yet, let the right person or people know you are interested so that your name is top-of-mind when an opportunity becomes available.

CHAPTER 5
Create Your Own Opportunities

"You will never have a perfect roadmap. But if you can understand that, then you can move forward."

I spent the first few years of my legal career waiting for other people to hand me opportunities. This produced a lot of angst. As an intern at the North Carolina Court of Appeals, I developed a sense of entitlement: *Here I am, I thought, working for free. Surely, a judge is lurking just around the corner waiting to reward my selfless service with a clerkship offer.*

That offer never came.

I watched in dismay as students and new graduates outside of the Court were offered clerkships, despite consistently positive feedback on my writing and research skills and my willingness to work extra hours. I started to wonder if there was something off-putting about me. Was I too eager? Did my writing stink? Did *I* stink?

But with the benefit of hindsight, I realize that I wasn't the problem at all. At least, my *work* wasn't the problem. I, as a *person*, wasn't the problem. But my mindset was. I was waiting passively for someone else to hand me an opportunity that was my, and only my, responsibility to earn. I thought that landing a career-catapulting clerkship would be as simple as showing up and doing stellar work. But this is not how the world works. The calculus is not that simple. You can work hard, produce good results, and still not be chosen for a specific role or opportunity. This isn't bad. It isn't cruel. It's just reality.

It took me nearly three years of dissatisfaction with my legal career to question the paradigm I'd adopted since high school. What if we don't need to wait for someone else to make a way for us? What if we can be our own way-makers? What if we can create the opportunities we want? What if we don't have to convince someone else that we can handle a certain opportunity, task, or challenge in order to take it on?

If I liked writing, the law, and writing about the law, was a judicial clerkship the only way to merge those interests? Could I manage to think outside of the (very small) box that is the legal industry's entrenched mores about which career paths are most worthy, which ladders are most worth climbing?

In the end, I chose to create my own opportunity instead of wasting my productive years continuing to wonder why no one else was inviting me into theirs. And I'm so glad I did. If I hadn't, I'd probably still be waiting, more jaded and bitter than ever.

"Don't Be Afraid to Create Your Own Path."

Natalie Anne Knowlton is a bold and unapologetic advocate for access to justice (or "A2J"), a movement dedicated to developing policies to take down barriers to legal services for low-income or historically disenfranchised populations. Natalie's career path has taken several fascinating turns, including a stint working for the Institute for the Advancement of the American Legal System at the University of Denver (IAALS), and founding Access to Justice Ventures, an organization empowering entrepreneurs building scalable A2J solutions.

Natalie always felt pulled to study international law and human rights. She majored in international studies in college, though she never expected to channel her interests into A2J advocacy work. In fact, she told me that she initially wanted "nothing to do with the law" and resolved to be the first in her immediate family to *not* become a lawyer. Eventually, however, she discerned that a law degree would "give some teeth" to the type of international affairs work that intrigued her, and so she headed straight to the career path she'd sworn off for years.

Law school opened doors for Natalie, like an internship with the United Nations in Tanzania. But when she graduated, she felt a sense of dissonance: she enjoyed the work she'd been doing and felt pulled to continue her focus on international affairs, but all of her classmates were applying for judicial clerkships. "I kept wondering, *am I supposed to do that too?*" she told me. The prospect of pursuing a traditional legal role, even a prestigious clerkship, interested Natalie as little as it did when she first entered law school, but the peer pressure was undeniable. It took an intense focus on her original goal—continuing her international affairs work—to resist this pressure and seek opportunities in her areas of interest.

Around the same time, Natalie discovered a new organization, the Institute for the Advancement of the American Legal System at the University of Denver (IAALS), an A2J advocacy powerhouse. There was an open research analyst position, so she applied, interviewed, and accepted the offer they made her.

Taking a job with a new and untested organization felt risky, but this (calculated) risk paid off immensely: the role was dynamic and challenging in all the right ways. Working for a new organization brought unexpected opportunities for Natalie to largely define her own role and focus on the advocacy areas that interested her most. Her responsibilities ranged from empirical research to sharing information with national stakeholders, providing public comment on rules changes, task force and state bar committee work, and researching, writing, and speaking. She worked with courts, academics, practitioners, technologists, and reform advocates from around the country and developed a strong and extensive network. Before long, she became known nationally as a pioneer of the A2J movement.

Natalie recently pivoted again by launching, along with some colleagues, a venture focused on advocating for systemic reform in the legal industry. None of this would have been possible if she hadn't trusted her instincts and interests. Instead of applying for clerkships like the other "good" law students, Natalie let her curiosity guide her. Working in uncharted A2J territory allowed her to create her own path, study the causes that interested her most, and ultimately, make an even greater contribution to the legal industry than she could have by doing anything else.

This type of professional curiosity can germinate in law school, not just after graduation or upon entering the workforce. Natalie emphasized that law students should start by resisting the urge to hyper-focus on the Bar Exam. Instead, she encourages students to take the courses, clinics, and internships that intrigue them. This can lend valuable insight into the types of work that are most, and least, appealing.

"You'll waste your time if you end up somewhere you don't want to be," Natalie said. "So, don't be afraid to create your own path."

"I Had No Intention to *Not* Practice."
Shunta Grant is the founder of the popular Best Today® company and brand. She has helped thousands of people harness the power of intentionality and routine through her products and courses. Her most popular product is the Best Today Guide, a 14-week planner and goal-setting guide, but she also hosts the Best Today Podcast and offers a variety of courses and products through her online shop.

When she graduated from law school, Shunta worked as a litigator at a large regional law firm. Her path was what she called "a continuation of a story of a girl who was competitive...and really loved arguing and being right!" she said, "which is what got me into law in the first place." Shunta's career roadmap was simple and straightforward: litigate, teach at a law school, then become a judge. "I had no intention to *not* practice," she said.

But when she had her first child, a daughter, in 2013, Shunta started to think differently. "The demands [of my job] became unreasonable," she said. She started exploring other, more flexible job opportunities, but nothing piqued her interest. It wasn't the subject matter of each job that concerned her; it was the quality and pace of life she would lead if she took any of those jobs, and she struggled to identify a path in the legal industry that would complement her new role as a mother.

With a waning interest in practicing law and a desire to find a creative outlet to keep her sane in the early days of motherhood, Shunta took what seemed like a sharp left turn: launching a hair bow company. Shunta started Because of Zoe (named after her daughter) as a side hustle in April of 2014, creating handmade bows and headbands for her daughter, then eventually for her friends and social media followers.

This creative side-hustle picked up steam quickly. As local demand increased, Shunta hung a digital shingle and started selling the bows online. Then, a local business asked her to sell her bows in their brick-and-mortar shop. Before she'd even realized it, Because of Zoe was so successful that by September of 2015, Shunta's hairbow revenue exceeded her law firm income. Sensing that she was onto something, Shunta resigned from her law firm to focus full-time on growing this new business.

People started asking Shunta how she'd grown a successful product-based business that replaced her law firm salary. Her answers to these questions unexpectedly pulled her into a coaching career. What started as providing one-on-one guidance to aspiring entrepreneurs eventually morphed into more official coaching appointments. This coaching work led to speaking opportunities, which brought in a steady stream of revenue. With more cash flow and increased demand, Shunta hired a team to help her reach more prospective coaching clients. Over time, she narrowed her niche, focusing only on women, and specifically, helping women manage their time and schedules through the power of routine.

Shunta initially intended to be a judge. But now, she's growing a successful online business. Instead of continuing to climb the ladder she was on, she stepped off the ladder temporarily to respond to her family's needs. This led her to a different ladder entirely, and she's been steadily climbing it ever since. It was a complete departure from her original plan, and her current business is not something she would have conceived as a young, ambitious law student.

"Even if you think you have a plan, you don't," Shunta said. "And I talk about planning for a living!" She admitted that lawyers, by their nature, tend to fear stepping off a predetermined path and departing from their plan. The risk of stepping away from that plan can, at times, feel fraught with unknowns. But it's impossible to weigh every possible risk and reward with limited data. Sometimes, the prudent course is to simply take a small step, then another, and another.

This requires becoming a bit more comfortable navigating uncharted territory, and accepting that pivoting might involve accepting a host of unknown risks, challenges, and rewards, *but that is okay.* There is a sweet spot in between recklessness and paralysis, and that is where we can move with courage and confidence.

As Shunta told me: "You will never have a perfect roadmap. But if you can understand that, then you can move forward."

Reflection Questions
When you applied to law school, what did you think you wanted to do with your career? Did that change at any point? What do you think catalyzed that change?

If your intended career path has remained unchanged, is that because your work aligns with your interests? Did you commit to a path because you felt like it was what you were "supposed" to do or because it gave you a sense of peace and security to simply choose something?

What would it feel like to imagine a different path for your career? Does it frighten you? Excite you? Does it feel audacious? Does it make sense?

How would it feel to step onto a path that involves more questions than answers, more risks than predetermined measures of success?

Action Step
Take some time to reflect on what you, or your family, need right now. Is it money? Is it flexibility? Is it the ability to work remotely

so you can be more available to tend to your family's needs? Whatever it may be, brainstorm small, micro steps you can take to satisfy those needs and to craft a solution unique to your particular stage of life. It can be very small, and it doesn't necessarily require cataclysmic change. It can be as simple as, for instance, requesting an additional remote working day, or taking on a side job (which we will discuss in an upcoming chapter) to increase your revenue.

CHAPTER 6
Set Your Tempo

"Even the most thrilling subject matter will fall flat if the tempo at which we're living and working doesn't agree with our temperament."

From an early age, we're asked what we want to "be" when we grow up. We respond by saying something like, *I want to BE a lawyer. I want to BE a doctor. I want to BE a college professor.*

Lawyers tend to respond similarly when asked about their intended career paths. *I want to BE an AUSA, a prosecutor, an appellate litigator.* But not only is this construct inherently limiting (few could succinctly sum up their employment in a simple "be" statement), but it fails to recognize that satisfaction in our work depends not on what we tell people we *are*, but rather, on how we spend our days. What we *do*; not what our friends or colleagues think we do, but what we *actually* do.

I've heard several authors and speakers, most recently, the author, comedian, and mother-of-six Jennifer Fulwiler, refer to this ebb and flow of activity and rhythms as the "tempo of life." Her most recent book, *Your Blue Flame,*ⁱⁱ dedicates an entire chapter to this concept. Though her book is not directed to lawyers in particular, the concept of tempo is particularly poignant for attorneys who, by their very nature, tend to gravitate to high-stress, high-pressure work. But everyone is wired differently. Some people inherently crave a faster tempo of life, with a calendar packed with events, tasks, and opportunities, and work that presents challenge after challenge. Others tend to frazzle easily and prefer lower-pressure work and a slower tempo with more flexibility and freedom to control their workload and schedule.

Fulwiler argues that our tempo of life matters just as much, if not *more*, than the content of our work. Even the most thrilling subject matter will fall flat if the tempo at which we're living and working doesn't agree with our temperament.

Shunta, who we met in the last chapter, told me the issue of tempo has been instructive each time she's pivoted. Her advice is to think about someone who you know is deeply unhappy in their work. "It probably has to do with some choice they've made that's affecting *how* they live out their days," she said. She told me that she wished more professionals would think beyond what they want to *do* or *be*, and instead, consider how they want to structure their schedules. She told me that she wanted to create a life that "doesn't feel like there's a fire all the time." This doesn't mean that she has no responsibilities, but it *does* mean that she has created a daily environment that complements her temperament, her unique wiring, and, most importantly, what works for each season (and its corresponding demands). A part of her mission at her company, Best Today®, is to help others to the same.

In law school, we're conditioned to just forge ahead, to do the work on our plates, and to not give much thought to how we are holding up emotionally, intellectually, physically, or spiritually. But these periodic personal assessments matter. If we are living and working at a pace that doesn't agree with how we are wired, we set ourselves up for massive burnout. It's worth taking the time to ask yourself not just what you want to do, what you want to be, but how you want to *live*. In a world (and a profession) where there are innumerable ways to earn a living, it's simply not worth charging ahead along a path that makes us miserable.

Reflection Questions

What's your preferred tempo? To help you discern, here are a few questions:

- Do you prefer consistency or variety in your schedule? Has this answer changed throughout your life? What is your answer right now?

- Do you need solitary time to think and process? Or do you work best while surrounded by other people? If you feel yourself saying, *well, I need a little of both*, think about what you would choose if you could only pick one type of environment. Which one could you not do without?

- Do you like being given assignments or do you prefer setting your own task list?

- Do you perform well with the pressure of a billable hour requirement or does that make you break out into a cold sweat?

- Do you like a fast pace, or do you need time to mull over your cases and projects? Do you get bored when there is down time? How do you handle last-minute assignments? Can you manage the pressures involved in little-to-no preparation time? Or do these types of situations make you anxious?

- How important is freedom, autonomy, and flexibility within your daily life? What would you be willing to give up in order to gain more control and freedom over your schedule?

- Examine your personal and professional circles. Whose lifestyle makes you feel a twinge of envy? What do you find yourself glamorizing? What are the particulars about their lifestyle that appeal to you most?

Action Step

Take some time to do what I call the "Ideal Day" exercise:

Imagine an ordinary Tuesday one year from now. Write out what your ideal schedule would look like, starting with the early morning hours. Pay special attention to the small details: Where are you sitting? What types of tasks do you tackle first when you open your laptop? Who is around you? Are you traveling?

Meeting clients? Working quietly in your home? Are you going to court? Are you negotiating deals? Who is calling or emailing you? Are you going into a physical office? What are you doing in the evening hours? How are you recharging? How do you feel? What is your energy like?

It is absolutely acceptable if your responses to these questions feel aspirational right now. Try to answer them as honestly as possible. This will lend valuable insight into what you want your days, your tempo, to look like.

CHAPTER 7
Stop Procrastiplanning

"Discerning what we enjoy, what we do well, and where we have the most potential for long-term career growth and longevity demands trying and testing."

As a new lawyer, I twisted myself into an angst pretzel trying to figure out what I wanted to do with my life. I distinctly remember bellyaching about my existential crisis with a group of fellow (unpaid) interns at the North Carolina Court of Appeals when one younger intern piped up that there was really no way to divine your interests out of thin air. "You just have to start doing stuff," he said.

I don't think he realized how profoundly this flippant statement impacted me. He had figuratively smacked me on the back of the head and pulled me out of my pity party. His statement inspired me to act, and frankly, I still think about it today when I feel tempted to wring my hands about where I'm going next in my career.

I call the tendency to overthink, over-plan, and over-reflect "procrastiplanning." Unlike traditional procrastination, it's especially dangerous because it *feels* productive. Aren't self-reflection and introspection inherently good, after all?

Well, yes…until they aren't.

Action Produces Clarity

It's easy to paralyze ourselves by ruminating on our greater contribution or higher purpose, our "Capital C Calling" as one of my friends calls it. As my fellow intern said, sometimes you just have to start trying "stuff" to see what catches. Particularly in the legal field, where the learning curve is steep, boots-on-the-ground experience has a way of both highlighting our natural talents and underscoring our limitations.

For example, as a litigator, my work at a small law firm showed me my natural strengths (writing, communicating, researching) and also made one of my natural limitations (fearing, and often avoiding, conflict) painfully evident. It's up to us to decide whether we want to confront those weaknesses and use them as growth opportunities, or pivot and pursue a career that involves fewer opportunities for those weaknesses to surface. As a litigator, I faced a choice. I could work to transform myself into someone more able to withstand antagonistic circumstances, or I could look for work that involved far fewer opportunities for high-conflict interactions. There is no "right" decision across the board, and there's value in both approaches. But with the benefit of hindsight, I can clearly see that I was correct in choosing the latter. It's not that my work now involves no opportunity for conflict or interpersonal challenges; it just involves a whole lot less of it. It's a better fit. And I wouldn't have known this if I hadn't *tried* working in litigation. If I hadn't *tried* pivoting into something else.

Discerning what we enjoy, what we do well, and where we have the most potential for long-term career growth and longevity demands trying and testing. It requires constant movement.

The lawyers I met when researching for this book hail from dramatically different backgrounds, but they all have one trait in common: they are thriving now because at some point, they decided to take the first step in the direction of curiosity, creativity, possibility. They started moving and they never stopped.

- Jeff took a job with Citigroup and volunteered to take on roles beyond his job description. This emboldened him to connect with a legal tech CEO, which led to a steady stream of ghostwriting opportunities, which opened a door to his current position with UniCourt.

- Natalie took a chance on a new organization and eventually launched her own organized committed to increasing access to justice.

- Shunta chose to spend more time with her growing family, which led to a creative hobby, which morphed into a product-based business, which funnelled her into business coaching, which transformed into Best Today®.

These careers were not born through top-down planning. They resulted from responsiveness to unique needs and acceptance of new challenges. They were the fruit of calculated risks and prudent micro-pivots. They happened through *trying* and *testing* different jobs and roles and organizations; through enduring situations that were a less-than-ideal fit, and embracing the learning and growth opportunities they presented.

Reflection Questions

It's time to stop over-planning. It's time to start acting. To do this, you have to figure out what's stopping you. Often, serial over-planning is rooted in fear, for example:

- Fear of failure (If I try to move in the direction of something new, what if it flops? Will people in the industry think I'm stupid or reckless?).

- Fear of success (What if I make a change and it actually works out? What will that demand of me? Am I prepared for a heightened challenge?).

- Fear of abandonment (What if no one supports me? What if the legal community ostracizes me?).

- Fear of sunk costs (What have I worked so hard for all these years if I'm just going to "throw it all away" to do something that may or may not even require a law degree?).

- Fear of judgment (What will people say? Will they think I failed in my current job and that's why I'm looking elsewhere?).

- Fear of disapproval (What about my parents/spouse/mentors who helped me get to where I am? Will they be disappointed in me? Will they wonder why I abandoned such a valuable degree? Will they think I wasted the time they poured into helping me earn it?).

Do any of these fears resonate with you? Why?

What would it feel like to give yourself permission to be curious about this new interest, new desire, new path, new opportunity?

Action Step

Choose one item from the list below, and tackle it this week.

- Set up an appointment with your law school career services office to discuss J.D.-adjacent career options.

- Say yes to that pro bono opportunity or volunteer role that sounds intriguing but that you don't feel you have time for. Are there ways you can get creative with your schedule to make it fit?

- Ask your employer if you can be assigned to a new case/team/ project that looks interesting to you.

- Assign yourself an exit date for your current role. Be realistic: if you have no idea where you are going next, then a six-month exit plan may not be practical. One year or 18 months might make more sense. Devise a realistic timeline and write it down. Consider this exit date a promise that you will not remain stuck.

CHAPTER 8
Find a Confidant

"If you're not happy, tell someone."

I'll never forget how I felt sitting over chips and salsa at a local Mexican restaurant with a woman in the legal industry whose career path I admired (and envied). It was the first time I admitted to someone outside my family that I wanted to make a career change. I was extremely nervous. Navigating this career transition felt like walking a tightrope between boldly seeking what I wanted but also respecting those who were currently supporting me. I didn't want to sound ungrateful for my current employment situation, yet I also wanted to make it clear that I was open to exploring other opportunities.

It felt audacious to discuss my still-developing career goals in such a public venue with someone else in the legal industry. But I knew I could trust this woman, and it felt incredibly comforting to confide in someone who knew me professionally, knew my employers, and yet, could relate to my desire to design a different type of life. She didn't dish out practical tips, but rather, assured me that I was not alone. It was cathartic to share, in a measured and professional way, that I needed a change.

Our conversation assured me that I could, indeed, prudently pivot. I had the strength, the motivation, and most importantly, I had family, friends, and local bar colleagues who would support me.

An Economy of Trust

Megan Sherron is the Assistant Dean of External Relations at Campbell Law School in Raleigh, North Carolina: her law school alma mater (and mine!). Megan was one of many bright lights at the law school. She was always smiling and upbeat, a welcome contrast to the anxiety and exhaustion that often permeates law schools, especially during exam season.

Two years after I graduated from Campbell Law, I ran into Megan at an admitted students' event at the school. I volunteered to attend the admitted students' luncheon and give a brief talk to the prospective students about my career and what had led me to civil litigation. I was starting to regret my readiness to volunteer. Unhappy as a litigator but not yet able to see another path forward, I slapped on a smile and did my best to convey satisfaction in my chosen career.

Before my talk, Megan and I casually chatted about life and work, I think she could sense that I was not being fully honest when I told her how much I enjoyed litigation. She told me that when she was a litigator at a local law firm, she often wondered if there were other options for her, if things would get better. It turns out they did.

I remember fighting back tears as I smiled and said something like, "I'm so glad it worked out for you." I wasn't yet ready to admit that I, too, was yearning to take a different path, but had no idea where to start.

I thought about Megan's words (and her career story) frequently throughout the following months. I started to realize that although I'd chosen a career that was a poor fit, I didn't have to keep trying to wear that ill-fitting garment. Megan had made a seismic career shift and yet still succeeded. Her path gave me a small glimpse into Life after Litigation, and I really liked what I saw.

From Campbell Law, to Litigation, to Campbell Law

When Megan graduated from Campbell Law in 2010, the economy was still reeling from the Great Recession, and job prospects were slim. "You were just excited to *get* a job," she told me. When she finally landed a position at a civil litigation firm with a strong local reputation, Megan counted herself lucky. She liked her co-workers and the case work was challenging and intellectually stimulating, but she couldn't help keeping one eye open to other opportunities. Sensing that litigation was not a suitable long-term option for her, Megan strategically confided in a few colleagues that she was interested in taking a different path if the right opportunity presented itself. This was a delicate balance since her employers were so connected in Raleigh. Megan had to walk a fine line, and she chose her confidants carefully.

This approach paid off. Two years later, the then-Dean of Campbell Law reached out to Megan to share a job opportunity at the law school: an alumni relations position that perfectly fit her extroverted personality. Megan jumped at the opportunity. It was, in fact, the perfect fit for her. And best of all, she was able to return to her law school alma mater, which she loved, and where she was already deeply connected.

Megan worked for the alumni relations office at Campbell for several years before being promoted to her current role as Dean of External Affairs. Her role has shifted and evolved over time, but it has always allowed ample space for her to grow and develop as a professional. Accepting this role, however, required a bit of a paradigm shift. Like so many other lawyers who pivot into a non-traditional career, Megan had to convince herself that it was okay to try something new, something outside of the traditional legal path.

"You put all this time and energy into law school, and you feel like you're going to disappoint other people if you go a different direction," Megan told me. "I was afraid I'd disappoint *myself.* Like taking some other option would be less-than. But I can worry about what others think, or I can enjoy what I'm doing. And I really like what I do."

This last part is key: Megan ultimately had to do the self-reflection necessary to knowing what type of day-to-day work would best suit her. "I had to sit down and think, what is it going to feel like to do this every single day? Will this be energizing, or will I walk away every day feeling mentally, emotionally, and physically drained?" For Megan, this meant taking a bit of a left turn out of traditional practice. What she found wasn't a "lesser" option to practicing law; it was a better option *for her*.

And yet, her time spent in traditional legal practice wasn't all for naught. In fact, the advocacy skills Megan honed in her two years working as a litigator still show up in surprising ways.

"Advocacy is not limited to a trial practice," she shared. "It's in all aspects of what we do as lawyers, and as people."

Spark Clandestine Conversations

If you take only one piece of advice from this book, let it be this: *if you're not happy, tell someone*. People won't share opportunities with you unless they think you're interested. They cannot read your mind. If you're silent, people will assume you're happy where you are.

It can feel scary to voice, out loud, that you're unhappy in your traditional legal job. However, the last thing you want to do is isolate yourself. Find someone you trust to keep your career aspirations private. It can be enormously helpful to run your ideas through the filter of a prudent, experienced professional, ideally, someone who knows you and has your best interests at heart.

Here are some suggestions:

• Meet with people in different industry niches or practice areas.

It's surprising how much you can learn from people whose paths are radically different from your own. This type of engagement will help you expand your mind beyond the traditional advocacy track that many law schools push.

- Schedule informational interviews. People love to talk about themselves and will usually oblige, particularly if you offer to pick up the lunch or coffee bill. A simple, "I'm really interested in what you do and want to learn more about it," can go a long way. These types of interviews can also create a web of contacts. One meeting can lead to another, and one introduction can spark five more.

- For those interested in working in higher education like Megan, think broadly. Some career options include general counsel, student services, career services, Title IX coordination, diversity and inclusion, admissions, alumni relations, fundraising, and adjunct teaching.

- Commit to saying yes to new opportunities even if they feel like a radical departure from a traditional legal path. You will likely find yourself using your legal skills in ways you never thought possible, but in a manner that complements your personality, interests, and skill set.

Reflection Questions

Who do you identify as a confidant? Can you trust this person to keep your career aspirations confidential while you discern your pivot?

Does this person have any connection to your current employers? If so, would it prudent to confide in this person, or should you look outside of your organization?

Is there anyone outside of you're the legal industry you can trust to share advice and wise counsel? Though their advice will not pertain directly to navigating the legal job market, is it possible that they have more general professional knowledge they can share?

Action Step
Identify the person (or people) you trust to hear, receive, and protect your career goals. Schedule a time to speak with this person (or people), candidly, about your goals, desires, and hangups. At the end of the meeting, ask them for one more contact in your area(s) of potential interest for your pivot.

Each time you meet with someone, continue this practice of asking for one more contact. Before long, you will start to build a web of contacts, each of whom could help you land your next opportunity (and you may be able to help them in the future, too!).

CHAPTER 9
Identify Your Work Personality

"It's vital to pause, reflect, and take stock of who you are. Of what drives you. Of what sucks your energy, and what recharges it."

Are you a *systems* person or an *individuals* person? In other words, do you thrive when working from a slightly detached, big-picture perspective, like engaging in policy work? Or do you prefer one-on-one, personal connections? Another way to pose this question is: do you tend to think in terms of the *system* or in terms of serving *individuals* with unique challenges? Are you wired to push for systemic change or to sit down with the person in front of you and work through issues one at a time?

If, in law school, you secretly prayed that your senior law clinic clients would no-show so you could work on a research project instead, don't work for a small law firm representing plaintiffs in high-conflict cases (ask me how I know). But if the idea of working on policies makes you feel detached from individuals and their human issues, then broadly speaking, you might be better suited for client-facing work than a corporate role or agency position.

A Systems Approach

Zacharia (Zack) Demeola is the Senior Director of Strategic Initiatives for the Law School Admissions Council (LSAC). He's a systems person, fundamentally motivated by a desire to address and correct the inequities within the legal industry. Yet he started his career in Big Law, because he excelled in law school, and thus was told he should "take advantage" of his high GPA.

Unfortunately, Big Law was a fundamental mismatch for Zack's personality, which was geared toward bigger-picture, systemic challenges and problem-solving rather than the highly detail-oriented work of litigation. Zack tried to push through his frustration with his work situation by taking on more pro bono cases, hoping this would diversify his workload a bit. It did, but it wasn't enough to keep him rooted at his law firm long-term. After a few years, it became abundantly clear that he needed to start looking elsewhere, even if that "elsewhere" meant taking a massive pay cut.

Zack stumbled onto his new career path in legal policy through what he calls "borderline desperation." When he saw an opening for a job with a new organization called IAALS, the Institute for the Advancement of the Legal System at the University of Denver (recall this from Natalie Knowlton's interview a few chapters ago), he felt inexplicably pulled to apply. IAALS was dedicated to civil justice reform, and it was seeking an experienced lawyer to do the work. It was a perfect fit for Zack. Though he was unfamiliar with the organization, it sounded good enough to him to throw his hat in the ring, and so he did.

"I wrote an impassioned plea in my cover letter," he said. "It was the first time I'd been myself in a really long time. I was just very honest about why I was so miserable."

His impassioned plea reached the right ears: IAALS offered Zack a position, and "everything changed." Reform work absolutely enlivened Zack. It was challenging in all the very best ways and like his litigation work, required the competitive desire to fight for change. It also demanded sharp, analytical thinking and practical solutions to meet real needs, all skills that Zack had developed in his Big Law career. And yet, as he explained to me, it gave him a lifestyle that was "sustainable."

"It brought in all that I'd loved about litigation, but without the misery," he said.

Zack's five years at IAALS were a time of intellectual and creative flourishing. He developed an aptitude for systemic analysis and human-centered design, specifically, studying the inherent inequities in the legal field that ripple across society at large. This work planted a seed: Zack started to feel pulled to work that focused on reforming these systems. And so, after spending a few years directing projects, seeking grants, forging collaborations with lawyers, courts, and academics, and working across the various teams in IAALS, Zack pivoted again. Now, he works for LSAC—one of the major gatekeepers of the legal profession. LSAC is the organization that administers the Law School Admission Test (LSAT), but it also offers support across the legal professional pipeline, from prelaw to practice, with an eye toward systemic equity and diversity.

Zack's role with LSAC is expansive. Currently, he is working to develop new products and services to support students, law schools, and new professionals. He is also leading a research initiative to better understand how to improve legal education and address inequity or lack of diversity in the education pipeline.

Like his role with IAALS, Zack's day-to-day work at LSAC fits his temperament and his wiring as a "systems" person. Yet this is an insight he developed only in hindsight. Because he excelled in law school, as a young lawyer, Zack was convinced that Big Law was his best and most prestigious option. It wasn't until he had been in the workforce for several years that he realized, "I should've gone into policy right off the bat." But this wasn't his fault, nor was it due to a lack of introspection on his part. As Zack said so aptly, law school is designed "to send the best and brightest to the best firms." For some, this might be the best choice. But for those who aren't wired for Big Law, it can be incredibly mind-opening to realize that there are equally prestigious, fulfilling alternatives to that traditional legal track. "I had options I didn't even know were available to me," Zack told me.

For law students, new lawyers, and mid-career professionals alike, Zack said, "it's vital to pause, reflect, and take stock of who you are. Of what drives you. Of what sucks your energy, and what recharges it." Ultimately, this is about knowing what type of person you are.

"You have to figure out what it means to stay authentic to yourself," Zack said, "because no amount of money is worth staying stuck and threatening your physical, mental, and emotional health."

And if you end up in a role that *does* start to threaten your health?

"Just know," Zack said, "you are never trapped."

Stop Feeling Guilty About Your Wiring

Every job will involve tasks that don't thrill you. But it's important to be honest with yourself about the type of work that drains your energy. When I was practicing law, I felt guilty admitting that I didn't enjoy working directly with clients. I had a hard time walking away from work that, on the outside, was so objectively meaningful. But presenting an emotionally drained version of myself to clients who really needed help, all because I'd convinced myself this was the work I *should* be doing, helped absolutely no one.

This is akin to a primary care physician feeling guilty he wasn't a brain surgeon because there were people with life threatening brain injuries who needed help. If I ever need brain surgery, I absolutely prefer a surgeon who loves his work over one who went into brain surgery out of some misplaced sense of duty. As for me and my client angst, who was I to think I needed to be the one to solve their problems when there are throngs of lawyers who are not only willing and able to do this type of work, but also, uniquely gifted in a way I simply am not?

A certain line of work may seem particularly worthy, impressive, or dignified, but this doesn't mean that you have to do it. *All* work is dignified and worthy when done with integrity and excellence, particularly when you align your unique skills and talents with the market's needs.

Reflection Questions

Are you wired to work for *systems* or *individuals*? To figure this out, try the following exercise:

- List all the work interactions, clients, and projects you've managed thus far in your career.

- Circle the ones that made you feel energized. Strike through the ones that sapped your energy, frustrated you, or gave you anxiety.

- Do you see patterns? Which ones are systemic or big-picture in nature, and which are tailored to one-on-one human interaction and personalized problem-solving?

- Take a talent inventory. Pull out your recent performance reviews from your job (this can include positive reviews from your clients).

- Do you see any patterns in these external assessments of your skills and talents? Condense these into specific personal strengths, specific points of contribution. Consider these points evidence of your wiring, your natural strengths.

Action Step

Google "J.D.-preferred" jobs. Read some of the job descriptions and lists of required skills. Which ones align with your talent inventory? Save them in a Google document or jot them down in a notebook. You will be returning to them when it's time to apply for a job or prepare for an interview.

SECTION 2

Logistics

"In a chronically leaking boat, energy devoted to changing vessels is more productive than energy devoted to patching leaks."
—*Warren Buffett*

CHAPTER 10
Build a Sustainable Lifestyle

"Live with less and you have more. You have more time.
More joy. More peace."

In 2020, the ABA Young Lawyers Division shared a study revealing the resounding impact of law school student loans on new graduates. The study aptly deemed the collective student loan burden a crisis. More than 75 percent of the survey respondents reported having at least $100,000 in student loans upon graduation, and more than half had more than $150,000. Unsurprisingly, the report revealed that these loans are negatively impacting lawyers' mental health.[iii]

Like thousands of other law school graduates, my husband and I shared a substantial student loan burden upon graduating, so my pivot required some creativity. Many (well, actually, most) of the alternative J.D. resources I read frustrated me, as nearly all of them were geared toward Big Law associates who had accumulated savings *and* swiftly paid off their loans. *Of course*, I thought, *I could travel the globe or open a cupcake shop if I'd been earning a high-six figure salary for a decade. Or if my spouse had a big fancy Big Law salary.* Their options looked wildly different than mine as a younger, much lower net-worth individual whose liabilities far outweighed my assets.

But that wasn't the problem: the real problem was that I wasted time complaining and hand-wringing about my situation when I could have been mapping out my options, and to be honest, I regret burning up so much of my energy on unproductive grumbling. All it did was inflame frustration and resentment toward everyone from my husband to my friends who were financially better off.

This negative feedback loop sucked my creative energy and threatened to slowly transform me into a negative, bitter person. Before I could make meaningful progress in my career, I needed to address this negativity and shift my paradigm. I needed to stop comparing my situation to my friends'. I needed to stop blaming the realities of my financial situation for my feelings of professional inertia and stagnation. And I needed to convince myself that feeding a despairing mindset would not only destroy my chance at reinventing myself professionally, but worse, rearrange me into a person I absolutely did not want to become.

And yet, while it's admirable to set goals and intentions for our careers, we also live in reality, and finances are a part of that reality. Even without the added burden of student loans, most people cannot afford to quit their job the minute they start to feel a hint of dissatisfaction. So, how do we allow ourselves to envision a different career path while staying responsible, prudent, and grounded in reality?

Pivoting Doesn't Mean Poverty: From General Counsel to Successful Wellness Coach

Tea Hoffman is the founder of Law Strategy Coach, the legal industry's premier provider of soft skills training for lawyers. She is also a sought-after speaker.

Before starting her company, Tea served as the General Counsel of a publicly-traded company, an unlikely portal into her massively successful career as a coach. In her work with hundreds of law firms across the country, it quickly became apparent to Tea just how little lawyers knew about the *business* of law. This inspired her to write and publish a book, *The Proactive Practice*, addressing some of the top business development issues facing lawyers. The book led to speaking and teaching opportunities for various state and local bar associations, making Tea an in-demand spokesperson for law firm business development nationwide.

In her burgeoning writing and speaking career, Tea continued to see a dearth of business development opportunities for lawyers and few professionals committed to helping them learn how to find (and sustain) business. To address this gap in the market, Tea started selling training programs based on the principles she taught in her book. Eventually, a large law firm purchased one of her training programs and asked her to create a business development department for their firm. It was this offer that launched Tea's coaching career.

Tea went on to earn a business coaching certification and started talking to the attorneys at that firm about their most pressing concerns. She was surprised to learn that overwhelmingly, the greatest challenges the lawyers faced were not related to business development, but rather, issues of personal satisfaction, fulfillment, and wellness. "They didn't know how to manage their lives," Tea said. "It became apparent to me I took the wrong course: I needed to be doing life coaching, not business development coaching."

Tea was flexible enough to respond to this need instead of insisting on progressing down the same path. She sought additional training and education and eventually became certified as a life coach and then, subsequently, a health and wellness coach. Her business continued to evolve as she moved into helping lawyers not just increase their revenue and gain more clients, but "stay in the practice longer…and be happier doing it."

The transition was far from seamless. Pivoting from running the legal department of a publicly traded company to coaching lawyers meant walking away from a salary that soared close to seven figures. Her husband was a police officer, so she was the higher earner by several orders of magnitude. Her family ended up selling their home and making seismic shifts in their lifestyle to accommodate Tea's massive salary decrease. But despite some temporary growing (or, rather, downsizing) pains, it was worth it. "[As General Counsel,] I never saw my kids," Tea said. "At some point, there was a tipping point. I could say, *hey, I can continue to make more money.* But at what point is that all worth it?"

Like many other professionals seeking to make a change, Tea faced the tension between two goods: a profitable career that provided more than enough income for her family, and greater flexibility, opportunity, and creativity. She was forced to weigh the opportunity cost of pursuing her own coaching, writing, and speaking opportunities against the loss of her massive salary and the prestige that came with it. The calculus wasn't easy, but it ultimately worked out in Tea's favor. She now runs a successful company and has crafted a sustainable long-term career path. And though her salary has not quite reached general-counsel level, she still does quite well, proving that a career as a creative, soft-skills-focused entrepreneur and financial success are far from mutually exclusive.

Tea's call to lawyers is simple, though certainly not easy, and arguably counter-cultural: *don't create a life that becomes impossible to manage.* "Lawyers have this stark realization of, *I hate this, but I cannot do anything else,*" she said. But she went on to explain that in many cases, professionals craft a lifestyle that matches their salary and status, and so when circumstances call for a change, they feel stuck. Some refer to this as the "golden handcuffs" phenomenon, the idea that you can unwittingly limit your options by embracing the abundant lifestyle that a healthy income affords. Yet difficult as it is to execute, there is an antidote: resist the urge to build a life that matches your income. If you suspect that you might want to pivot, live beneath your means. Cultivate a lifestyle that leaves some margin so that when you need or want to make a shift, you can. And if you've already built that abundant lifestyle, confront what it might mean to walk away from it, to radically downsize everything from your home to the other privileges you enjoy. Can you still find fulfillment if you live on less? What do you really, truly need?

"Live with less," Tea said, "and you have more. You have more time. More joy. More peace."

Tea acknowledged that this is not an easy choice. But the key is recognizing that it *is* a choice. Cultural norms can be powerful and persuasive. When the company we keep maintains a similar level of privilege and material abundance, it can be difficult to admit that there are, indeed, other ways to live. We have the power, and the responsibility, to choose a path that feels appropriate for ourselves and our families.

"You have to decide," Tea said, "how you want to live the rest of your life."

Reflection Questions

Are you prepared for a different lifestyle than the one you are currently living?

What are you willing to sacrifice in order to transition into the type of job you'd like?

If your pivot involves a pay cut, what can you remove from your budget's bottom line to accommodate that reduction in monthly cash flow?

What does "success" mean to you?

Action Step

Schedule a meeting with a financial advisor (some insurance companies and banks of whom you are already a client may provide these services for free) to review your assets and liabilities and your current financial plan, if any. Develop a realistic and practical picture of your financial situation and what, if any, room it allows for potential increases or reductions in your pay.

CHAPTER 11
Make Your Job Your Patron

"I had all this energy to create, and try, and learn."

Can't just quit your job on a whim? Join the club. We're a thick tribe, those of us who rely on an income to survive. But instead of lamenting our financial realities, can we get creative?

When I wanted to leave my law firm, I didn't have much financial leeway. I knew I couldn't afford to leave my job to focus on my freelance writing business, but I also couldn't pursue that type of work *while* working for the firm. Some pivots may be perfect as a side hustle until you can grow them into a standalone income, but since mine would involve taking on other local law firms as clients, I could only start my work after leaving the firm.

I needed to find a workaround. I needed to find a patron.

The Patron behind My Business

The book *Real Artists Don't Starve*[iv] by author, speaker, and entrepreneur Jeff Goins introduces a concept that entirely changed the way I thought about my financial situation. I paraphrase Goins in saying that, if we want to pursue work that inspires or energizes us, we need to cultivate *patrons*. And a job can be a patron. This means that while you are working on your pivot, whether that involves learning a new practice area, growing a business, taking a course, or studying for another Bar exam, our current job can be the steady source of income we need to keep us grounded while we grow.

In December of 2017, I put this patronage concept into action for the first time. I contacted a document review company located in an adjacent town (about a 25-minute drive from my home). Two of my friends, who were also in a transitional period in their careers, worked there as they discerned their next steps, and they encouraged me to apply. With their help, I identified a contact with the company and sent her my resume. Within two weeks, I'd been assigned a desk and a company email account. I spent the next five months reviewing documents in a large warehouse by day and working on my business at night. It was enormously comforting to nurture my fledgling business knowing that if it failed, or if I simply had a bad month, I could still rely on the document review income to land in my bank account. Starting a small business was certainly risky, but with the steady stream of income that document review provided, it was a risk that wouldn't send us spiralling into bankruptcy.

When I started the document review job, my goal was to drop down to part-time as soon as possible so I could focus more time and energy on growing my business. I set my income goal, and once I landed three recurring monthly client accounts, I cut my hours from 40 to 20. Eight months later, I replaced my law firm salary, and I quit document review to focus full time on Davis Legal Media.

Though many lawyers looked askance at my decision to quit a good job at a respected firm to "do doc review," I credit my time at Dauntless Discovery for abundant personal and professional growth. As a litigator, I suffered from crippling anxiety. Taking time away from such stressful work to do much easier, lower-stakes work while growing a business that excited me allowed the stress levels in my body to dissipate. As my health improved, so did my energy, and as my energy increased, my business (and, as an added bonus, our family!) grew.

Sometimes, the changes we yearn for happen exactly when they're supposed to, even if we would've chosen a different path for ourselves at the outset. I wouldn't have initially chosen such a roundabout path to motherhood and entrepreneurship, but my story unfolded exactly as it needed to.

This unfolding will continue throughout the rest of my life. And it will continue throughout yours, too.

Start a Side Hustle
Robert Ingalls is the founder and CEO of LawPods, a podcast production company serving the legal industry. Just a few years into business, LawPods is producing podcasts for some of the largest

law firms in the world. Robert's success stemmed from a series of intentional, unglamorous pivots.

Robert practiced law for nearly seven years, starting out in criminal defense before eventually moving into civil litigation. Though he enjoyed trying cases, Robert had no idea how to make real money, manage his time, or find healthy ways to cope with the stress unique to the legal profession. This lack of alignment fanned the flames of the anxiety he perennially struggled to manage. After a conversation with his wife about their future, their plans for their family, and their ongoing financial concerns, Robert realized he needed to figure something out, and soon. If he was going to support his growing family, he needed to start making real money. And if he was going to start making real money, he needed to get a handle on his stress and anxiety. The way that he'd been living and working simply was not sustainable.

Instead of buckling down and trying to scale his solo practice, Robert chose the lower-stress option of document review. He kept his law practice open and continued to take on cases, mostly meeting with clients in the evenings, to keep his options open. But document review became his main source of revenue, providing a sufficient stream of income for his family while buying him time to discern his next step.

Document review opened a pressure valve for Robert. With a reliable source of income and less stress, he was able to finally sit down to compile a list of priorities. At the top of the list was finances. Robert knew he needed to get his family financially solvent, and so with his newfound mental clarity, he began to consume books and podcasts about finances while he reviewed documents. He then moved on to podcasts about business management and entrepreneurship.

This steady IV-drip of content energized Robert. The more stories he consumed about people who had created fulfilling and profitable careers out of whole cloth, the more he started to believe that he could do the same. He started to shift his mindset, which had been stuck in his law practice: his focus had been on squeezing more money out of his legal work, instead of the numerous directions that he could take his career instead.

At the same time, Robert began to fall in love with podcasting as a medium. "I was amazed at how these shows could give me so many ideas," he told me. After a few months, he decided to try to create his own podcast, so he set up a makeshift podcasting studio in his spare bedroom. After reviewing documents all day, he'd come home and plan, record, and produce shows.

"My wife thought I was crazy," he said. "I was high. Everything in my brain was just clicking and moving, and I had all this energy to create, and try, and learn." Though he didn't yet know that one day he would make a living as a podcast producer, he did love the work of creating his own show and the access it gave him to the professionals he interviewed about their stories and lives.

As energy and movement beget more energy and movement, later that year, Robert signed up for a podcasting conference. There, he connected with other professionals who were just as excited about podcasting as he was, and he came home invigorated. His fire for podcasting burned on, but there was still one small issue: money. His document review job was keeping his family afloat for the time being, but he knew this was not a long-term solution. He needed to find a way to provide for his growing family while stoking the fires of his passion for podcasting.

This discernment eventually led Robert to apply for and accept an entry level compliance position at a bank. At this point, he had been slowly winding down his law practice and eventually closed its doors, thanks to the influx of income from his bank job, which paid much more than document review. But unlike his civil litigation practice, his new position was still flexible enough to allow him time to work on his podcast and even teach a podcasting class at a local coworking space, which gave him connections in the industry where he wanted to stay long-term (someone from the class became his second client when he started LawPods).

At that point, progress accelerated. Robert shifted from producing his own podcast to responding to requests to produce podcasts for other lawyers. Shortly thereafter, he started to promote his podcast production services, and these one-off jobs eventually bloomed into what is now LawPods.

Within a few years, Robert was able to support his family on the income he made from his podcast production business and now, he and his team are producing shows for firms like McGuire Woods and Skadden Arps. His concerns about finances are a distant memory, and he spends his days immersed in work that energizes him and is valuable to the legal industry, a true win-win.

"It's amazing," he said, "because none of this was predetermined. All of it was getting up every day and deciding to do something, try something. I used to live in this box where you did something a certain way. Now, I just do things."

Reflection Questions

Would your employer allow you to take on a side job? If not, are you willing to leave your job and look for something else that can provide a steady stream of income while you pivot?

What are five side-jobs you would be comfortable doing?

What type of work does your lifestyle and schedule allow? Are you able to work at a physical office, or do you prefer a remote working option? Are you able to take on contract legal work, or would this potentially pose a conflict of interest?

Are you willing or able to leave your 9-5 to do something like document review if it would allow you to pour your time and energy into growing your business, sharpening your skills, applying to jobs, or otherwise working on your pivot?

Action Step

If you are truly ready to leave your job to work on your pivot, it's time to act. Send your resume to 10-15 different part-time or full-time jobs that would give you enough income to release some pressure while you figure out your next steps.

If you would rather stay in your current job while you work on your pivot, figure out who, in your office, you need to contact to determine whether it is possible for you to moonlight, take a class, launch a business, or do whatever is necessary for your specific pivot goals. Granted, most employers won't take kindly to an employee who starts whispering of their desire to leave the company or firm, so try flipping through your HR materials or employee handbook, if you have one, to see if there are any provisions about what type of outside work is permissible during the course of your employment.

CHAPTER 12
Cultivate Humility

"There is no shame in saying 'I don't know'."

In my religious tradition there is a prayer called The Litany of Humility. Ask any Catholic about this prayer and you're likely to elicit a heavy sigh or an eye roll. We all know it's good for us, but it is intense, essentially a very long list of prayers asking God, in no uncertain terms, to bless other people abundantly and to let us be okay with being completely forsaken. It's been said that this prayer is particularly efficacious, so needless to say, no one's in a big hurry to pray it.

Though the professionals represented in this book hail from a broad diversity of cultural and religious experiences, they universally agree that humility is a wise yet shameless teacher.

Humility is a virtue worth cultivating if you intend to make a professional U-turn. Moving into a new or unfamiliar industry will mean subjecting yourself to a steep learning curve, which can sometimes feel like a skills regression. You may find yourself tasked with responsibilities that feel "beneath you" as you learn your way around your new organization, company, or role. As you do this work, remember that in any role, we cannot be trusted to do big things until we prove faithful in the little things, no matter how many letters follow our names.

In one of my law school classes, the professor brought in outside speakers to discuss their career paths and answer questions about everything from the post grad job search to navigating a challenging office culture. One week, a visiting lawyer told us about his experience working for a law firm in small town North Carolina: his very first job out of law school. A partner at the firm wanted to treat everyone to lunch at a storied hot dog joint in town. Apparently, these hot dogs were legendary, and the boss wanted to ensure everyone in the office had a taste. This newly-minted lawyer was the one tasked with picking up the hot dogs. When he returned to the office with the food, his boss asked him to cut the hot dogs into pieces and distribute them to everyone in the office. To add insult to injury, he even asked him to reheat the hot dogs in the microwave first.

So here he was, a new lawyer who'd spent three years in law school and an entire summer studying for the Bar Exam, only to find himself microwaving hot dogs. I remember this man telling his story and saying something like, "at that point I wanted to just say, *screw this, I'm not doing this anymore.*" But he didn't. He warmed up the hot dogs and he stuck around.

Recently, when I was chatting with one of my law school classmates about this very story, he told me that he knew the hot dog associate and apparently, both he and the boss eventually moved on to another organization. Now, the roles have been reversed: the boss directly reports to the hot dog associate. The associate's hot dog delivery days are more than a distant memory. I often wonder if the same would be true had he refused to cut the hot dogs. Probably not. He would likely still be cutting hot dogs, just somewhere else, having been assigned entry-level status after spending a career telling anyone who would listen what types of assignments were beneath him.

When I find myself wrapped up in some mundane aspect of my job, I say to myself, *hot dogs*. As this lawyer was formed in the furnace of a humbling office culture, I, too, can be refined by willingly accepting tasks that feel beneath my pay grade.

Regardless of our station, we should all expect to warm up hot dogs from time to time when that's what the office needs.

"Shut Your Mouth and Open Your Ears."

Jennifer Mencarini is the Director of Diversity and Inclusion at a large law firm, a path she never could have envisioned as a young attorney litigating medical malpractice cases. Yet no matter how many steps she climbed on the professional ladder, Jennifer's misery only grew. "I could never figure out why I was so good at being an attorney but it was so bad for me," she said.

After too many years of trying to force satisfaction in her legal career, Jennifer eventually chose to pursue a master's degree in human rights and social justice, a path that better aligned with her personal and professional interests. As a part of her studies, she went on a civil rights pilgrimage and met a well-known activist in Selma, Alabama. This fortuitous meeting ignited Jennifer's passion for diversity, equity, and inclusion in the workplace. Though she didn't yet know she'd eventually devote her career to these causes, she felt pulled to learn more about patterns of injustice in her community.

"I felt in my heart that this was something I needed to pay attention to," she said, "even if I never did it for pay."

After a divorce that shook her family emotionally and financially, Jennifer started looking for jobs in higher education that would support her. She happened to stumble upon a job posting in a law school career office. Though it wasn't specifically focused on diversity, equity, and inclusion, which she would have preferred to pursue as a career, she knew it would get her in the door of academia and allow her to start building experience in that new environment. She applied for the job, was made an offer, and accepted.

Jennifer's job description was specific and clear, but circumstances called her to a different role, one that fell outside the bounds of what she'd initially agreed to do. When the law school reeled from the pain of a disturbing, racially-charged incident within its walls, a piece of Jennifer's prior work experience in multicultural student affairs at a university came into play. She was asked to serve as a resource for students, faculty, and administration as the community worked together to heal individually and collectively and create improved support structures for historically underrepresented community members.

"I didn't know what I was doing, but I had to figure it out," she said. "I had to make myself available and keep showing up. If I made a mistake, I had to fix it and move on."

This new role demanded a lot of Jennifer. She worked hard to build relationships and understand the wildly different needs of the students who sought her counsel. Most of all, she had to learn how to admit, again and again, that she was still learning, still figuring out how to meet everyone's needs, still navigating the treacherous terrain of high stress and broken hearts: a posture that, in many ways, runs counter to our wiring as lawyers.

"Lawyers are always told to *fake it till you make it*," she said, "that you have to portray that you know what you're talking about, even if you don't. But that's a mistake," Jennifer explained. "There is no shame in saying *I don't know*. It's worse to fake it because this is not authentic or true."

Jennifer leaned heavily on her community in learning to speak honestly and open herself up to critiques, even if they were deeply painful and humbling to hear. But in any role, humility is a muscle worth strengthening. Sometimes, she said, our responsibility as professionals is simple: "Shut your mouth and open your ears."

"Nobody Cares What I Think Anymore."
When John Boswell accepted his position as the Chief Operating

Officer of the international non-profit Zoe Empowers, he was fresh off of a nearly thirty-year career in the private sector. The former Chief Legal Officer of a very large, privately held software company, John now oversees a global network of local organizations supporting orphaned children and vulnerable youth. Globally, Zoe spends most of its time and resources providing vocational training for children in small communities and also educating them about their legal rights. The organization's cause, and John's role within it, has essentially nothing to do with the private sector work he enjoyed for nearly three decades, but it is enormously fulfilling.

John's connection to Zoe started through volunteerism. He served on Zoe's board of directors without any plans to eventually work for the organization. But as he approached thirty years of work in the private sector, it became apparent to John that it was time to make a shift. Though he had enjoyed his work, particularly as Chief Legal Officer, he inexplicably knew he was being pulled to explore something radically different for the remainder of his career.

Right around the time he discerned it was time for a career shift, John "coincidentally or miraculously" heard from a friend who was connected with Zoe. "He said, *look, I know there's no chance you'd do this, but I'd like you to consider it,*" John told me. And though it was entirely unfamiliar terrain, John accepted.

As COO, John primarily fills two roles within Zoe: about 80 percent involves fundraising, and the rest is managing the handful of U.S. employees and the more than 70 employees who are based overseas. When John first accepted this position, he was suddenly a beginner, a status he had not had for decades. "When you are the boss," he said, "every pearl that comes out of your mouth sounds intelligent." But, he explained, when the power dynamic shifts and you're no longer respected for who you are, for your role, "you have to get things done through the quality of your ideas, not just because you said something."

This, he shared, was one of the most significant points of his professional growth when he accepted his role with Zoe. The mission is larger than any individual person or executive, no matter how vital their role in the organization.

"I realized," John said, "that nobody really cares what I think anymore."

Reflection Questions

Think about humbling moments in your past. What happened? How did these moments make you feel? How did they help you grow?

As uncomfortable as it was to be humbled, would you subject yourself to that situation again if you knew it would help you grow personally and professionally?

Who are some people in your personal life who exude humility? What is it like to be around these people? How do they exhibit humility?

Who are some people in your organization who you would define as humble? What is it like to work with them? What specific qualities make them a good leader? A good co-worker? A service-minded professional?

Are you prepared to be a beginner again, or to start from a lower rung on the ladder, if you pivot? How does this prospect make you feel? What emotions does it elicit?

In a similar vein, if you are taking a pay cut for your pivot, does that make you uncomfortable? How and why?

Action Step

Take some time to reflect on your answers to these reflection questions. Then, write down every trade-off you will have to make if you pivot in your career. Will your pivot involve a pay cut? A title that feels less prestigious? A new universe of information and skills and people that makes you feel like a beginner all over again?

Consider whether these trade-offs will be worth it to you. Can you handle less prestige, pay, or professional confidence if you are also less stressed, stuck, or frustrated? Do you think you could find excitement and opportunity in the challenges?

Take these questions, and your responses, to someone you trust and who knows you well, and discuss it together. Sometimes, the ear of a person who knows you well is the very best filter.

CHAPTER 13

Find a Hook

"The opportunities that opened for me didn't happen because of any particular legal skill."

Something that causes a lot of anxiety and grief among young lawyers is the *how do I make myself marketable?* problem. The *all the jobs require experience, but how do I get experience if no one will give me a job?* problem. There is a workaround, and it involves finding some small connection that closes the gap between your current work situation and the work you ultimately want to do.

John Boswell, who we met in the last chapter, describes this as "finding a hook." This is the process of looking for something, *anything*, that connects your bank of knowledge, skills, and experience to the job you want.

If you take a deep dive, you'll likely find *something*: a point of experience, knowledge, or passion that connects you to the job, that will ignite a spark of interest in a hiring manager. Recall Jeff Cox's story from earlier. He was fresh out of law school when he interviewed for his role at Citigroup. Though he had no work experience yet, he presented a research project that exhibited his capacity to gather, analyze, and synthesize data, one of the job requirements. Instead of waiting to be asked about his proficiency in data analysis, Jeff showed up to the interview with his research project already in hand. He took initiative and made the interviewers' job easier—an excellent way to start a professional relationship!

John Boswell shared his perspective as a professional who has hired scores of young lawyers. "Don't just go in and say, *I know nothing about this job but I can work hard and learn.* Find some way to get experience in the specific industry or role, because otherwise, you'll never get past the HR manager who's reviewing the resumes. Go get something that you can put on your resume that demonstrates you have that skill set."

John raised the hypothetical example of a young lawyer who wants to work for a computer software company, but his only work experience thus far has been in criminal defense. This lawyer could create his hook by joining the technology section of his state bar association to immerse himself in the language, news, and trends in that industry niche. Then, he could apply to work part-time for a small software company so he can add to his resume, *served as outside counsel for a software company.* As John said, even if the "company" is a guy in his garage with a dream and a vision, this would be a very persuasive, strong hook. It demonstrates sustained interest in the industry and a commitment to learning about it. It demonstrates real, tangible, articulable skills. It *shows*, rather than *tells*, a hiring manager that this particular lawyer is hungry to learn.

Once you find your hook, lean on the power of the personal connection. Comb your network, John said, and try to find a contact in your target company who can vouch for you and draw attention to your hook. John explained that hiring managers are more motivated by the fear of making the *wrong* hiring decision than the desire to make the *right* one. These people are under a lot of pressure, so a character reference from someone in-house can mean the difference between a swift rejection or an interview. The personal recommendation makes you seem less risky, and can get you in the door even if your resume is not as persuasive as it could be.

When I applied for my first legal job, my employer hired me (fresh out of law school) instead of someone with five years of experience. This was only because two prominent people in our local bar *personally* vouched for my character. I had zero proven, demonstrable skills to offer, other than my overtures in my interview about "how hard I work" (cringe) and my "hunger to learn" (double-cringe). The founding partner of the firm later confided that they chose me because of these character references. (I imagine my interview "skills," if anything, were a liability rather than a boon.) You can teach skills to a newbie, he explained, but you cannot teach character. And so, as a young attorney with no experience yet, my hook was knowing two people who were willing to promote me.

When my husband applied for his current job, his hook was an intimate knowledge of one particular niche area of law. The mechanics of his prior job looked nothing like the work he would be expected to do in his new role (he was a courthouse magistrate applying for a policy-heavy job in the bill drafting division of our state legislature), but he packaged his neutral position and his knowledge of this highly specific area of law as an asset to the organization. He explained to them how the unbiased role of a magistrate is not very unlike that of a nonpartisan bill drafter. In the end, the interviewers agreed, and he was able to move from being face-to-face with criminal procedure and courthouse operations to examining those very same subjects from a ten-thousand foot view.

But, you might wonder, *what if I can't find a hook? What if I'm new to the local area, the bar, the community, and I don't yet have any character references to boost my credibility?*

I'm glad you asked.

Your Law School Education Means More Than You Think
A senior executive at a large legal technology company gave me his secret to conquering barriers to entry: "Don't underestimate the education you get in law school," he said. "It may not seem applicable when you first come out of school. But in hindsight, having been a lawyer for almost thirty years now, it's actually really relevant." He went on to explain that law school teaches you to "break down problems, to see two sides of a problem," and in a corporate context, "that's hugely important."

This executive also shared that his company hires many students right out of law school because he and his fellow executives recognize that "there are so many things you can do with a law degree that have nothing to do with a large corporate practice." Again, you can teach the particulars of a specific job. What you cannot teach, and what matters most, is the raw material: character, and three years of training in critical, analytical thinking. Thinking "like a lawyer."

Decades ago, this senior executive made his own dramatic pivot out of private practice. In his law practice, he made a habit of volunteering for opportunities that no one else wanted, for instance, international travel and working in a niche practice area. This eventually led to a position with a different organization, where he met the person who would ultimately vouch for him when he applied for a role within his current organization. Now, he negotiates multi-billion-dollar licensing and procurement agreements for some of the world's largest companies.

This executive's career path proves that sometimes, your greatest asset is your willingness to do what no one else wants to. This, alone, can open doors. This, alone, can be your hook.

"The opportunities that opened for me didn't happen because of any particular legal skill," he told me. "It was about me being interested in travel. Me being interested in taking on complex problems. Taking on special projects," he said. "It was all about pushing myself outside of my comfort zone and doing things that other people weren't willing to do. All the times I've done that…those are the highlights of my career."

Reflection Questions

Review the job description for the type of role you want. Write out the requirements, vertically, on a piece of paper. Then, in a separate column, write out each and every one of your job responsibilities in your current role. Leave nothing out: include even non-legal or quasi-legal roles you take on in your firm or organization.

Then, review each column. Do you see any items that look similar? (For help, re-read the chapter on Reframing Your Role).

If, after doing this exercise, you still can't find a hook, how can you create one? Can you seek out a certification or take a class to learn more about your target industry? Can you do something tangible to go *get* the skills you'd need for the job you want? For instance:

- If you want to learn about marketing, can you become HubSpot Inbound Marketing Certified?[v]

- If your target industry is software, can you ask to shadow someone who works for a software company, take a coding class, or join your local bar association committee on law and technology? Can you start such a committee if your local bar doesn't already have one?

- If you want to break into the non-profit world, can you volunteer for an organization that promotes a specific cause? Can you serve on a non-profit's board of directors or serve as a consultant for an organization that interests you?

- If you want to be a writer, can you start a blog to showcase your skill? Can you launch a newsletter or podcast on the niche practice area, topic, or industry you want to learn more about? How about pitching an article idea to an industry publication, or contacting an industry leader to offer to ghostwrite?

Action Step

It's time to create your hook. Give yourself about two weeks from the time you've read this section to figure out yours. Review the questions above and choose one item to tackle. If it's joining a committee or registering for a course or certification, figure out whose permission you need within your current organization. If it's making a connection in your target industry, comb your network to find someone who fits the bill. If it's writing or speaking on a particular topic, go ahead and buy the domain name for your website, order a microphone for that podcast, or start that Google document to keep track of your notes, thoughts, and article drafts.

CHAPTER 14
Become Uncomfortable

"You have to make decisions without all
the facts in front of you."

Growing up, whenever I faced an unpleasant task, my dad would quip: "This will require you to become uncomfortable." It was a phrase he'd heard from a colleague, who'd heard it from his coal-miner father, and the implication was clear. Many things in life, no matter whether they're essential to our livelihood or a natural part of personal growth, will require us to become deeply uncomfortable. My dad has taught me that dodging discomfort is a fool's errand. To live richly, we need to learn to not only manage a bit of discomfort, but to expect and *anticipate* it.

Pivoting is uncomfortable. At some point in your transition, you'll have to resign yourself to some unglamorous grunt work. Making the decision to pivot is easy, but taking the steps needed to successfully transition into a new role or career is much more difficult.

The executive we met in the last chapter shared his perspective on the power of welcoming discomfort. "You have to embrace change," he said. "Don't be afraid of it." He went on to explain that in the legal field, younger lawyers have the advantage of witnessing, in real time, various changes that are constantly unfolding. This helps them develop a baseline level of tolerance for frequent disruption.

This executive also shared that his own career path had little to do with luck or opportunity, and much more to do with boldness in seizing opportunities to test out these new ideas, technologies, tools, and opportunities, even when doing so felt audacious and even unsettling: "Try things outside your comfort zone," he said. "If you're interested in legal tech, take some coding courses. See what you enjoy. Try lots of things. Do what feels intimidating. And then, the practice of law becomes fulfilling."

Be a Beginner Again, *Again*
John Boswell told me that when he first started working for Zoe, he had absolutely no idea what he was doing and was constantly overwhelmed. His overwhelm stemmed not from his workload or responsibilities, but from the fact that he was operating very far outside his comfort zone. As CLO of a privately held company, there was no issue that he hadn't already seen and addressed. But with Zoe, everything was new. "All the things I thought would work were stupid," he said. "I realized I wasn't as smart as I thought I was."

Yet even for a seasoned professional like John, these learning curves were not new. Early in his legal career, John would often seek advice and counsel from other lawyers who were more experienced in a certain practice area, thinking that they would surely draw from a much deeper well of knowledge. But he eventually learned that, ultimately, "all we're doing is applying our best efforts and no one actually knows the absolute answer." This taught him that professional success, is more about repeatedly seeing an issue and testing out solutions, not necessarily intuiting the right answer every time.

"No one is smarter than you; they have just dealt with something you haven't," John told me. When he was a young lawyer in the private sector, struggling to internalize this truth, he realized that he needed to keep working to refine his skill set and to broaden—and deepen—his knowledge. "I realized, I'm not the best at this, but I'm not the worst, either. What I don't know, I will learn."

And it takes a lot of time to reach this comfort level. John shared that it took him about 15 years of work in the private sector to reach a level of expertise where nothing surprised him, where he felt supremely comfortable handling virtually any issue. He also worked alongside a seasoned group of lawyers, so whatever he didn't know, they did, and he could draw from this bank of collective wisdom. Yet when he pivoted into his work for Zoe, he once again stepped into refreshingly uncharted territory.

"It's about just being comfortable with being uncomfortable," he told me. "It's nice to be put in your place every now and then. You don't know anything. You're just a knucklehead."

No One is Going to Die on the Table

Tyler Roberts is the founder of NOMOS Marketing, a full-service marketing agency for lawyers and law firms, based in South Carolina and serving clients nationwide. Before launching the company with his wife in 2018, Tyler worked as the Associate Editor of a national legal publication. He hails from a journalism background and always saw himself as a writer, so it wasn't a surprise that working in-house reviewing contracts fresh out of law school wasn't quite scratching his creative itch. A confluence of personal and professional needs eventually pushed him to resign from his job and pursue writing and editing full-time. "Even though it involved a pay cut, it was worth it," he told me. The pivot not only saved him from a long commute that was steadily wearing him down, but also gave him the creative freedom he desperately wanted.

At the same time Tyler transitioned into a creative career, his wife was working for a marketing agency that served the dental industry. Tyler and his wife had become good friends with the owners of that agency, another husband-and-wife team, and they began to discuss the possibility of working together one day. They'd considered what it would look like to replicate their business model, which had been successful in dental, for the legal industry. After spending some time discussing the potential risks and rewards of a new entrepreneurial venture, the two couples took the leap together: using the infrastructure of their current agency, they launched NOMOS Marketing.

NOMOS started as a small operation—consisting of its four original founders—but now, they've onboarded a team and serve law firms across the country from their South Carolina office. In the company's early stages, Tyler worked hands-on with law firm clients to create marketing plans, design websites, and craft content. Now, he has pulled himself out of the day-to-day of serving clients and moved into a different role as CEO. Some days, this work involves managing his team. Others, it's setting up health insurance or 401ks. Granted, these are dramatically different skill sets. But Tyler sees it as ultimately connected.

"You have to trust the process and be flexible to adapt and pivot when needed," he said. "Whether you're practicing law or running a business, it's the same evolution. You're exploring all the things that can possibly go right, you're making plans, plans don't always go how you hoped, and then you have to adapt."

Granted, lawyers are conditioned to be hyper-aware of risks, which Tyler admits can produce a high level of anxiety that can make it difficult to act, to take calculated risks, and to be flexible enough to test different solutions. But with entrepreneurship, he added, "you have to make decisions without all the facts in front of you." This reality is particularly difficult for lawyers to swallow. We seem to have been stamped from infancy with an aversion to making mistakes. This makes sense, given that in legal practice, mistakes can lead to angry clients, malpractice claims, and lost cases—which can be a (literal) matter of life and death. But in business, typically, no one's life is at stake, so you can afford to make a few mistakes as you climb and eventually master the learning curve. For lawyers who are accustomed to operating under tremendous pressure, this truth can be enormously freeing, even if it's deeply uncomfortable for us to admit as Type A, high-performing perfectionists (okay, maybe not all attorneys fit that bill, but it's a stereotype for a reason, and denial's not just a river in Egypt).

But as a friend of mine said so aptly, most of the time, when we mess up, "no one is going to die on the operating table."

Reflection Questions

Does the prospect of pivoting make you uncomfortable? If so, how or why? Does the discomfort of pivoting outweigh the anxiety or unhappiness, if any, that you feel in your current role?

Think of a time in your life when something made you intensely uncomfortable. How did you approach that task or event? What did it feel like to face it head-on? What happened? What did you learn? How did you grow?

Surveying the past few years of your career, has your tolerance for discomfort increased? How so? What do you think has helped you become more comfortable with being uncomfortable?

Action Step

This week, do one thing that makes you uncomfortable. It can be as small as speaking up in a meeting or volunteering to handle a hearing. It can be something much larger, like signing up for a leadership role in your local bar, enrolling in a course, or asking for career advice. Challenging ourselves requires the use of muscles that can atrophy if we don't engage them enough, so the key is to find simple ways to strengthen them.

CHAPTER 15
Stop Waiting for Your Big Break

"Careers aren't made in big breaks. They're made in small steps, micro decisions, pivots, mistakes, triumphs, and breaking points."

Many working professionals tend to think about their careers in terms of big breaks. We think, *if only I can get my foot in the door here, or if only I could catch this person's attention…then, I'll really set myself up for success.* And so, rather than creating opportunities for ourselves, we wait around for other people to create them for us. To give us permission. To write our ticket. To open doors and usher us through.

Lawyers are particularly susceptible to this mindset. Ours is a hierarchical, merit-based profession in which reputation matters deeply and personal connections are king. We are wired to think that if we can just earn the good graces of the most prominent, powerful people in the industry, then we will write our own tickets to wild career success.

But careers aren't made in big breaks. They're made in small steps, micro decisions, pivots, mistakes, triumphs, and breaking points. As Robert Ingalls (of LawPods) says: the "little things" we do every day turn into the "big things."

Robert's path to successful entrepreneurship is living proof of this mantra. When he hit an exceptionally low point personally and financially, he took the small step of attending a podcast conference. There, he met other podcast enthusiasts who convinced him he, too, could make a living as a content creator. And though he overflowed with ideas on how to launch his business, he decided to pick one pragmatic step: accept an entry-level job doing compliance work at a bank so he could pay the bills while he learned the ins and outs of the podcasting industry, which was where he really wanted to land. Two years later, Robert's business earned more than enough revenue for him to quit his bank job.

Robert didn't wait for someone to notice him, praise him, or give him permission to pivot. He took the time to figure out what he wanted to do. He took calculated risks. He broke into the podcasting industry and built his business prudently while still supporting his family with a job that supplied a steady, consistent source of income.

Small steps can feel frustratingly insignificant. But forward motion is forward motion. As an ancient Chinese proverb, usually credited to Lao Tzu, says: "The journey of a thousand miles begins with a single step."

Reflection Questions

Have you been waiting for your "big break?" Do you feel you've been more passive than active thus far in your career? Are you waiting for a permission slip? Are you waiting and hoping for someone to notice you and give you an opportunity?

If not, and if you have been more active than passive in seeking out opportunities, what, specifically, have you done? What metrics have you used to track your success in making connections, developing skills, or seeking new opportunities? How have you measured your progress?

Who are some people in your industry that you admire? What was their origin story? Did they experience a "big break" at any point? If so, what small steps did they take that ultimately culminated in professional success?

Action Step

Think back to one of your greatest accomplishments. Write it down. Then, write out all of the small steps that led to this success. Think about how similarly small, micro steps can lead you further down the career path you yearn to walk. As you write down these small steps, get as granular as possible. Whose wisdom do you need to seek? What do you need to rearrange in your life or your finances? What old, unhealthy thought patterns do you need to jettison?

Make note of everything that comes to your mind. Set your notes aside, and revisit them in a week, then a month, then next quarter. See if any of your thoughts, reflections, or responses change.

Make a regular habit of revisiting your notes as you continue to grow personally and professionally. Each week, each month, each quarter, you will likely notice yourself taking small steps to move your career or your long-term goals forward.

CHAPTER 16
Find Affinity Groups

"Instead of leaning heavily on any one professional mentor, join affinity groups, or groups formed around some common interest, that will connect you to the types of people you'd like to know."

I can still picture the weary looks in older lawyers' eyes when I introduced myself at local bar association events. They knew it was coming: the desperate plea for a meeting, an interview, a shot. In retrospect, I don't blame them for getting a bit exasperated. It had to feel demoralizing to disappoint lawyer after hopeful young lawyer, telling them that they simply could not promise a job to everyone who asked. I really hated feeling desperate, and I hated making them uncomfortable, and I also hated how annoyed they seemed by my very presence. But as a young attorney with few connections, I wasn't sure what else to do other than show up, smile, shake hands, hand out resumes, and ask (beg?) for opportunities.

Law schools tout the career-changing benefits of one-on-one mentorship. *Find your person, your mentor, your guide,* they seem to exhort students, again and again. They push students to identify that person who will take them under their wing and present them to the profession like prized livestock. But UniCourt's Jeff Cox, who we met a few chapters back, shares a much more effective networking approach: instead of leaning heavily on any one professional mentor, join affinity groups, or groups formed around some common interest, that will connect you to the types of people you'd like to know. This will expand your network, teach you about your areas of interest, and arm you with knowledge and connections you can take to job interviews. This type of involvement can provide your "hook."

Jeff recommends joining bar association groups that focus on the practice areas that intrigue you. Better yet, offer your time and talent by volunteering for a leadership role or spearheading a project. This type of active involvement with a group of like-minded attorneys is much more effective than chasing down a single lawyer and badgering him or her to take you to lunch. In one scenario, you are professional peers with these attorneys, building your relationship naturally as you collaborate with one another to accomplish common goals, while in the other, you are implicatively presenting an ultimatum upon which your entire relationship will rest: *will you help me or not?*

In a similar vein, Tyler Roberts of NOMOS Marketing recommends attending legal tech conferences and walking the exhibition floor, looking for like-minded peers. Each year, Tyler and his team travel to legal conferences and forge new relationships with other vendors, speakers, and attendees.

"I guarantee all those vendors are businesses that were either started by an attorney or have an attorney on staff doing sales or customer support," Tyler said. "All the people I've met who are doing really interesting work in the legal field are attorneys but are doing software sales or client services or writing books." Some firms or organizations may even pay for you to attend if you can make a compelling case that your attendance will bring a tangible benefit to the firm in the form of connections or new industry knowledge.

My business grew exponentially when I got involved with my local chapter of the Legal Marketing Association and developed relationships with other professionals in my industry niche. I have received sage advice and countless referrals from this group and now consider multiple members of the group to not only be colleagues but mentors and friends.

At the Intersection of Tech Tools and Legal Services
Jessica Demuth worked as a paralegal before law school. She wanted more from her career, so she pursued a law degree, but she was deeply disappointed when she took her first job as a litigation associate at a boutique law firm and did the same paralegal work—but three years and a massive financial commitment later. Disappointment coupled with the long hours and bombastic and ever-changing nature of litigation spurred Jessica to start speaking with recruiters about other options. She craved a challenge, yearned for a lifestyle that felt a bit more enjoyable, and longed for work that was more collaborative than solitary.

But instead of finding her an entertainment law job, which Jessica thought she'd wanted, the recruiters she met showed her the versatility of a career in recruiting. As an extrovert, Jessica learned that working as a recruiter would present more opportunities for connection, which her litigation job lacked. So as a bold departure from her original plan, she took a job as a recruiter, scouting contract attorneys to manage document review projects for her employer.

Before long, Jessica's work caught the attention of a recruiter for Major, Lindsey & Africa, the world's top legal recruiting company, and she made the switch to work for the corporate giant. In her new role, Jessica worked with law firms and corporations to fill various legal positions, including general counsel and assistant general counsel. Almost all of the recruiters were attorneys as well, and she learned that her legal background was enormously helpful when it came to placing candidates in the right roles given their background, experience, and the needs of the target company.

It was a long conversation with her boss, however, that led Jessica to her current role with Exigent Group, an alternative legal services provider (ALSP) company offering legal services and technology solutions for law firms and legal departments. She and her boss discussed the future of legal and where Jessica saw herself fitting in the industry. Jessica knew she wanted to be a part of the massive transformations taking place in the legal industry and that her background in law firm staffing translated well into the business development world. Her move to Exigent has allowed for all of this and more.

At Exigent, Jessica has taken on a legal operations role that lives at the intersection of tech tools and services. Legal operations is the marriage of law and business units.

Broadly speaking, those who work in this space manage an organization's legal budget and resources, implement legal technology and processes to improve efficiency, and liaise with outside counsel and other legal service providers. In her specific role, Jessica spends her days connecting with legal teams to find opportunities for enterprise impact. Fragmented procedures, poor visibility into contracts and terms, and inefficient, manual processes prevent legal departments from delivering value. Jessica's role is a part of the movement to streamline and improve the delivery of legal services by addressing these issues.

"I'm learning something new every day," Jessica told me. "There's always some new way to automate or enhance the practice of law in an efficient way. Legal tech is evolving and there is always a new tool or process to talk about, learn about, and implement," she explained. But putting new systems in place is just half the battle: you also need a human element, that is, someone to make the tools work within the firm's ecosystem. Jessica explained that this is precisely where legal operations professionals come into play.

"We all went to law school because we wanted to learn and understand things in a deeper way and find the why," she explained. A role like hers does just this: it keeps you sharp. It keeps you at the forefront of the industry, where the big problems are solved. It keeps you thinking and growing. You stay relevant. You stay helpful.

The legal operations space is rich with opportunities. Jessica's advice for lawyers who want to break in is to follow the people who are leaders in these spaces. Connect with them on LinkedIn, follow groups like the Corporate Legal Operations Consortium (CLOC), and attend conferences to explore the various tech vendors that are supporting law firms. Find a topic that interests you and learn as much about it as you can. Talk to recruiters. Ask other legal operations professionals how they broke into their fields.

A legal operations job opens doors to infinite learning opportunities and growth potential. For Jessica, a future could involve breaking away from her organization to serve as an independent consultant for law firms or legal departments, or she can work in-house as a director of legal operations. In a field that's constantly growing, so, too, are her options.

Young lawyers interested in exploring a career in legal operations can take advantage of the fact that many of the roles don't require prior experience. "It's more based on character," Jessica explained. "They'll train you on their specific technology tool, on why it matters and who needs it. But if you have a good temperament for sales, then you'd be a good fit."

She also said there's hope for the introverts among us who want to break in. "You can do more project management work or help build legal solutions internally. You don't have to be face-forward to the client if you don't want to!"

Reflection Questions

Have you relied on a single individual (or individuals) for help and guidance in your job search?

Instead of focusing on one person's counsel, can you expand your thinking? What opportunities are available with your state bar association? If there aren't any existing affinity groups for your area(s) of interest, could you start one?

Have you ever considered learning about legal technology and how it's revolutionizing the profession? Have you explored the different tools that your current firm or organization uses?

Have you thought about the future of the profession at large *vis a vis* your role in it?

Action Step

Pull up the website for your local or state-wide bar association and review the list of committees. Identify a few that spark your interest. Your homework for the week is to join one, attend the next meeting, and as a bonus, volunteer for a leadership role or offer to sit on a sub-committee.

For bonus points: schedule a coffee or lunch meeting with one of the new friends or colleagues you met through this committee.

CHAPTER 17

Reframe the Burden of Law School Debt

*"There are many ways to earn a consistent income;
we just may need to get a bit creative and flexible
about what we are willing to do."*

If you're serious about pivoting but like thousands of other lawyers, you're bogged down by law school debt, you may have to get creative—especially if your pivot involves a pay cut. You may have to take on a side job or cut expenses, but if pivoting is the right decision for you, it will be worth it.

Marissa Geannette is a former Big Law associate turned writer, author, and coach for young lawyers seeking to advance and succeed in top law firms. A few years into her career as an associate, Marissa started to sense that the partnership track at her firm didn't appeal to her. She wasn't sure exactly *what* she wanted to do, but she was confident that advancing at her firm was not her long-term goal.

While she discerned her next steps, Marissa committed to living as frugally as possible so she could pay down her substantial law school debt. She knew that financial freedom would afford her plenty of options if she could be disciplined enough not to build a lifestyle commensurate with her Big Law salary.

After about seven years at her firm and right before becoming eligible for partner, Marissa had paid off her debt and built a robust emergency fund. This allowed her to resign from her law firm, even though she did not yet have a plan for her next career move.

Armed with savings, a healthy 401k, and a clear head, Marissa took some time to discern her next steps. She started by taking a job at a gym, which allowed her to bring in some income while she launched and grew a blog, The Unbillable Life, a resource for Big Law associates seeking to thrive personally and professionally. With plenty of thoughts to still process from her seven years in Big Law, Marissa went on to write *Behind the Big Law Curtain*, a primer on how to succeed as a junior associate. "I had this theme of giving advice to my younger self, and thinking, *what would have been helpful for me to know as a junior associate?* So, I put all this material into a book."

As she worked on the book, Marissa took on freelance writing jobs and coached law firm associates on how to advance at top law firms. Although she enjoyed the freedom that self-employment allowed, Marissa admitted that she occasionally struggled to detach herself from her identity as a lawyer. "I didn't know what to call myself," she said. "I was never comfortable calling myself a writer. So, I just called myself a lawyer and hoped no one asked any follow-up questions!"

Recently, Marissa transitioned back into part-time legal practice. She found herself wanting to dust off the skills she'd honed in her legal practice, but she also wanted to take advantage of the increased flexibility lawyers are now enjoying in the workplace. Gone are the days when lawyers are tethered to a specific firm or organization. Lawyers can now cobble together income and jobs in a way that fits their desired lifestyle and their personal or familial needs.

Marissa started by making herself available for freelance legal work, which she could do from home and on her own schedule. She eventually found more steady work at smaller, remotely-based law firms and began to offer to work with them on a contract basis. This flexible model fits Marissa's lifestyle and interests. "I didn't know what my goal was for post-Big Law life," she explained. "But I figured out that I like many different things and I wanted the opportunity to try them all: writing, coaching, *and* using some of my legal skills." She went on to explain that her struggle with Big Law wasn't actually the legal work itself: "I just hated the constraints. I hated it controlling my life. I hated it being all that I was."

Marissa encourages young lawyers to find hope in the ways the legal industry is changing. Leaving a job is no longer a death sentence for your legal career. "You can leave, and you can always go back," she said. "I think people are now very understanding of those who take time off or try something different."

When she left her law firm, well-meaning colleagues told Marissa that she shouldn't be "running away" from Big Law, but "running toward" something else. "But this kept me there," she said, "unhappy.

For a long time. So even if you don't have a destination, it's still okay to leave something you don't want anymore," she said.

This approach worked for Marissa because she was proactive about keeping her expenses low and paying down her debt. But her lesson can apply universally. You can make a shift or a change even if your entire future is not mapped out. And so long as you keep your legal mind sharp and maintain your CLEs, you can return to the law, even if your legal career will look different than it did before.

And for those of us who may not have the financial flexibility that Marissa did (i.e., if we have debt but also dependents to clothe and feed), recall from Robert Ingalls' story the benefit of document review or other flexible employment situations. There are many ways to earn a consistent income; we just may need to get a bit creative and flexible about what we are willing to do.

Seeking Collective Wisdom

To chart her own path, Marissa admitted that she read "every book that ever existed about leaving a job or a career." Openly discussing her desire for change was taboo within her law firm circle, so she relied heavily on other professionals' stories to get a taste of what her life could be like if she explored other options. "A lot of lawyers need evidence ahead of time that something is going to work out," she explained. But when you're taking a bold step, you lack that assurance. That's where other people's stories encouraged Marissa. They provided empirical and anecdotal evidence that career shifts, even massive ones, are much more attainable than we think.

Above all, Marissa's advice is to make the choice that you feel pulled to, and to discard well-meaning but often sabotaging advice and opinions. "Not everyone will think what you're doing is valuable," she said. "But many will. And at the end of the day, who cares!"

Getting Creative about Finances

Marissa's path may not be an option for everyone. As we've discussed a number of times, if you have a family, for instance, you may not be able to live on a shoestring. Student loan debt can be a very real burden for lawyers who want to pivot out of traditional legal practice.

Fortunately, though, there *are* options. Some of them may seem unconventional or you may even feel a bit sheepish admitting to other lawyers that you've taken a unique path. But if you are truly feeling pulled to pivot, you can find a way to manage your debt and finances while growing in your career.

Though I urge you to meet with a financial planner who intimately understands the particulars of your financial situation, here is a brief sampling of some options for structuring or repaying your debt:

Income-Based Repayment Plans

Many federal student loan servicers allow you to adjust your monthly payments from standard repayment to an income-based repayment plan. This means that your monthly payments will remain proportional to your income. While this may not be an ideal long-term strategy (if your loan principal is large enough, a smaller monthly payment may not chip away at it nearly fast enough, or it may result in interest only accruing even faster), it can allow families to accumulate more savings, build an emergency fund, or work toward other financial goals. In a season where you're feeling particularly pressed financially, this could be an option to consider.

Public Service Loan Forgiveness [vi]

If you take a full-time non-profit or government job, you may qualify for public service loan forgiveness after 120 monthly payments, which would forgive the entirety of the remaining loan and interest balances of applicable federal student loans. Under this program, the forgiven amount is not considered taxable income, so you will not be stuck with a massive liability upon forgiveness. The catch? Your options are (somewhat) limited to public interest positions. However, the gamut of qualifying employers is broader than you might think, and it can even include work you did before entering law school if performed while paying off other federal student loans that were subsequently consolidated with your law school student loans.

Additional Revenue Streams

Many lawyers opt to take side jobs to pay down their loans. Adjunct teaching, tutoring, reviewing Bar Exam essays, or freelance writing, for instance, can help you earn another $20,000 or $30,000 annually to throw at your loan balance. Your employer may even allow you to take on a part-time document review position for an organization like United Lex, Consilio Services, or Hire Counsel, so long as it does not present a conflict of interest.

A few ideas for side hustles appropriate for lawyers are:

- Freelance legal work through Up Counsel

- Freelance legal writing or editing work for sites like LawClerk. Legal, Fiverr, or Upwork

- Adjunct teaching at a law school or community college

- Blogging for Clio Blog or Justia

- Transcribing audio from legal proceedings through companies like Transcribe.Me, E-typist, and Cambridge Transcriptions

Many lawyers (myself included!) have used a combination of the above to fund their pivots. There is absolutely no shame in any of these approaches. Do not let anyone even begin to hint that the path you've chosen is unworthy, and be protective: you should never feel forced to share, explain, or justify these professional decisions.

Reflection Questions

Are you willing to make simple or dramatic lifestyle shifts to make your pivot successful, given your current income, assets, and liabilities?

Is your spouse or partner (if you have one) on board with your plan to pivot? Is there anyone else in your life who can keep you accountable from both a personal and a financial perspective as you make this transition?

Are you willing or able to take on a side job to fund your pivot? Be honest with yourself about what you are (and are not) willing to do. It's easy to claim that you would do anything to get out of a tough situation, but be cautious, as they say, about jumping from the frying pan into the fire.

Action Step

Take a *post-mortem* of your financial habits for the past year. Track all of your sources of income as well as your expenses. Consider them in light of your long-term financial goals, for instance, saving for college tuition or retirement, investing, charitable giving, etc. This may seem a bit elementary, but it's vital to scrutinize our financial habits before making a massive change to our income. This is important whether your pivot involves a massive pay cut or, if you're lucky, a pay increase! Substantially *less* income means you need to do all you can to ensure that you and your family are still meeting your financial goals as well as your basic needs. Substantially *more* income may call for a more strategic approach to how you are using or investing your funds. Either way, you will need to fully understand every detail of your financial situation and whether, and how, you're priming yourself for long-term success.

SECTION 3

Mindset

"Knowing you need to make a change isn't enough. You've got to find the guts to do it."

— *Robert Kiyosaki*

CHAPTER 18
Reject A Totalizing Title

"I do feel like an attorney, because deep down, I really am. That's the beauty of this profession."

Mindset work is gaining popularity in the legal field. In the past year, I have spoken with several mindset coaches who specialize in working with lawyers. These conversations taught me that lawyers are a particularly challenging client population because the beliefs we carry about work, life, and identity are so deeply entrenched.

Our minds are extremely powerful. Through our thoughts alone, we can thrive and find peace, or we can unwittingly sabotage our own success. This is because our minds create an environment in which one, and only one, of two mindsets can incubate: one of abundance, or one of limitation or scarcity. We can assure ourselves that our options are as numerous as the stars in the sky, or that our degrees limit us to a discrete number of traditional legal career paths. We can believe in our power to pivot, or we can convince ourselves that change is either impractical or simply not worth the trouble.

This is not a plug for trendy buzzwords like "manifesting." Rather, the type of mindset work these professionals advocate is a simple paradigm shift from *I could never get from Point A to Point Z to I can definitely get from Point A to Point B. I can figure out how to get to Z later. But I'll never get to Z if I don't first get to B.*

We can find clarity through action. Through movement. Through intentional, small steps. No one can "manifest" a thriving career simply by making a vision board, hiring a coach, repeating mantras, or high-fiving themselves in the mirror (I'm not denigrating any of these practices, by the way. If they help you feel better, great.). But you can take one tiny step. Then another, and another. Small, micro shifts do eventually have a cumulative effect.

When I finished my interviews with the other lawyers represented in this book, I parsed my notes, looking for data. Before long, five common threads emerged, weaving their way through the pages like a serpent: five common, pervasive, limiting mindsets that plague lawyers and stymie their growth. Throughout my hours of conversations with other lawyers, it became evident to me that these blocks kept my friends and colleagues stuck for months, years, or in some cases, decades. In this final section, we're going to uproot each of these limiting beliefs.

More Than a J.D.

For years after I left my litigation job, when people asked me what I did for a living, I'd stumble around a clunky answer that inevitably started with, "well, I was...*am*...a lawyer..." I used my title to prop myself up, to lend legitimacy I felt I'd otherwise lack if I'd simply said, "I'm a writer." To this day, I admit that I still struggle to quell this strange impulse to make sure everyone in the room knows that I'm a lawyer. Upon reflection, I realized it is because I, like many lawyers, root my identity in my professional status.

I've met countless lawyers who've admitted to feeling similarly. They are nervous to walk away from the ever-satisfying descriptor of *I'm a lawyer*, no matter how miserable they are. And even after they pivot, they still feel pulled to preface any discussion about their work with the qualifier: *I am a lawyer by trade, but now, I do X, Y, or Z.*

Some of this could be due to pride, but I think there is also some legitimacy to this tendency to cling to our professional status. Lawyers are widely respected because the public generally understands and appreciates what it takes to become one. The title commands respect and does, indeed, say something about our intellectual capacity, mainly, our ability to consume and make sense of complex information. Nonetheless, we hold many different titles, statuses, and identities in our lives, and being someone who's earned a law degree is just one of them.

None of this is meant to diminish our accomplishments as lawyers. Rather, I hope to encourage you that should you choose to pivot in your career, you lose only a title. Your analytical mind will travel with you and may even be sharper and clearer when it is put to use in the right environment, wherever that is for you. Not to mention, clinging to a title instead of ardently pursuing work that is a better

fit will result in serious professional dissatisfaction. As I heard a
colleague say once, and I paraphrase, *being able to tell people what you
do for a living is not the same as living it every day.*

Stymied by External Expectations

Many lawyers fear disappointing those who helped them progress
along their professional path through law school and into the
legal field. In many cases, this fear makes pivoting feel almost
disrespectful to (or a betrayal of) those who've helped, mentored,
and guided us throughout our professional journeys. But these fears
are misplaced, and we need to fight, hard, to not let them guide us.

"One of the biggest mistakes people make is thinking they have
to follow a script and do what's expected of them," Tyler Roberts
(of NOMOS Marketing) told me. "But there are so many exciting
things happening in the legal profession. It's hard when you're a
young attorney because you're trying to build your reputation," he
said, "but it's okay to reframe the way you think about your career
options. Listen to podcasts. Read articles. Go to conferences. See
who's doing something different, and engage with them on social
media. Learn as much as you can."

We can engage in this type of ongoing education and discovery
while we are still in a traditional legal role. Even if we one day leave
the law entirely, the tapestry of education, experience, relationship-
building, and formation we've engaged in up to that point will
only make us better, stronger, more skilled professionals, no matter
what we do for work. And those who've worked hard to support
and guide us along the way will celebrate the ways we've put our

education and experience to use. Those who care the most about us want to see us thrive, and committing to a lifelong process of curiosity, discovery, and learning is one of many ways to do so.

You Will Always be a Lawyer

One of the great benefits of earning a law degree is that once you're a lawyer, you're always a lawyer. Shifting your day-to-day work from practicing law to something obliquely related (or even completely unrelated) doesn't suddenly suck the legal knowledge out of your head. There is no Alternative J.D. Career Police Squad headed to your house to rip your bar license off your wall. If law school and legal practice shaped you, you will retain that shape. No matter what you do with your career, that will always remain an indelible part of your formation.

"I do feel like an attorney," Megan Sherron (the Dean of Alumni Relations at Campbell Law School) told me. "Because deep down, I really am. That's the beauty of this profession."

Don't Box Yourself into a Title

Since he graduated from law school, Josh McIntyre has worked in a variety of legal marketing and member engagement roles for non-profits. He previously worked in policy and network advancement for a national teacher's association, but recently, he's moved into a role as Senior Director of Outreach and Engagement for a non-profit called the North Carolina Advocates for Justice.

Josh's marketing, policy, and non-profit work stemmed from his experience litigating civil cases at a small law firm in coastal North

Carolina. It was immediately apparent to Josh that civil litigation was a poor fit for his personality. It wasn't the people, but the work itself, that left him feeling misaligned. Regardless of this obvious dissonance in his day-to-day work, Josh struggled to walk away from a job at a law firm because *being a lawyer* had become tied to his identity. But as Josh now acknowledges, this type of identity labelling is the fastest way to hamper the self-discovery required to find alignment. In his pivot from private practice into the non-profit sector, Josh took time to figure out what he liked about his job: personal connection and advocacy.

"I had to stop thinking about *the law* as a general, amorphous category, and instead, think about aspects of my job that I *did* like," he said. Thinking about his career options in terms of specific roles and responsibilities instead of labels and titles helped Josh get past his identity hangups and drum up the courage to apply for alternative J.D. positions. Once he landed his first non-traditional role as a regional representative for Kaplan Bar Review, Josh had set himself on a career trajectory that would give him more longevity. Departing from work that was a poor fit gave him the energy and clarity he needed to not only excel in his current role, but also, discern his next steps.

"It really did help change my life," he said. "I went from feeling burdened and dragged down and tired, to having energy and doing very well. I realized that those aspects of my new job not only brought me joy, but I could apply all of my new skills to my next job as well."

Reflection Questions

Do you feel tied to your identity as a lawyer? How would you feel answering the question, *what do you do?* with something other than, *I'm an attorney?*

What other identities do you carry? Are these identities professional, personal, or a mix of both?

If you step away from your title as an attorney, what would you lose? What would you gain?

Action Step

Here are a few factual statements. Read them, then write down the ones that resonate with you. Then write them again, and again, and again. The more you write them and reflect on them, the more you will start to believe that they're true.

- You are not just a lawyer. Regardless of its importance to society, the practice of law is a job.

- You are not limited to performing work that was unavailable to you prior to entering the legal profession. Your law degree expands your opportunities. It does not limit them.

- People who love and support you will not be disappointed when you make choices that are best for you or your family.

- If you choose to leave the law, you can always go back.

- Being able to tell people what you do for a living isn't the same as living it every day.

- You will not serve anyone well if you continue to operate from a place of burnout and misalignment.

- It is your responsibility to find alignment if you feel misaligned in your work.

- It is not selfish to admit feeling dissatisfied with your work.

- It is okay for your professional interests and goals to change.

CHAPTER 19
Think Beyond Meaning

"No matter what your job is, you can always make the world a better place either within your job structure or outside of it."

We are products of a meaning-obsessed culture. Research indicates that in particular, millennials (roughly defined as those born between 1980 and 1996) desire work that feels meaningful, to the point that they would willingly trade higher pay for a greater sense of fulfillment in their jobs.[vii] While there is nothing wrong with desiring work that feels meaningful, fixating on finding "meaning" and "purpose" in our work can often paralyze us.

A desire for meaning and purpose is what leads many compassionate, purpose-driven people to law school in the first place, goading them to believe that there is no better way to serve individuals in their moments of greatest need. Yet seeking to draw meaning from our work is expecting a lot of the workplace ecosystem. Should we really rely on our work to bring meaning to our lives?

I floated variations of this question to several lawyers. Their answers roughly fell into two camps. Some said, *yes, meaning in our work is vital.* Others said *no, you do not need to find your work meaningful, so long as you can find meaning somewhere else.*

One of the most compelling answers was from John Boswell (of Zoe Empowers), whose take was balanced: "No matter what your job is, you can always make the world a better place either within your job structure or outside of it," he said. "You can always volunteer on a Saturday morning to clean up the neighborhood, tutor a child, mentor someone. And this will make you feel better about yourself than anything else you do."

John's single caveat was this: go with your gut. "You can't work in an industry where it is hard to walk through the front door," he said. "Find the industry that you really enjoy talking about. If you do that, you'll get good at it. It's a positive feedback loop."

Tea Hoffman (of Law Strategy Coach) had a similar take. "Everyone needs to figure out their why," she said. To illustrate, she shared a story about the man who used to pick up her trash. Her driveway was long, and when they purchased their home, they knew that part of the deal was that they'd have to lug the cans to the very end of the driveway each week. But the very first day they moved in, the garbage collector made the trek down the long driveway on foot. He retrieved the cans, emptied them, then returned them, before turning around to trek back *again* to his truck.

One day, Tea stepped out to thank the man for going the extra (literal) mile. He told her he'd been doing the very same thing for years for the home's previous occupants. Waste management was his second job, he explained, the one that was paying for his three daughters to attend college. *It's all worth it,* he told Tea, *because I always think about how far my daughters are going to go in life.*

Did this man find deep meaning in his waste management work? Perhaps. But his *why,* saving enough money to send his daughters to college, gave him the energy to not only do the job, but to go above and beyond.

Connecting your work to a *why* will infuse it with purpose, even if the work itself doesn't drip with meaning. Matt Hrutkay, the wellness coach we met several chapters ago, shared his perspective as a former Big Law attorney who suffered from serious mental health issues. "It doesn't have to be all or nothing," he said. "Say, for example, you're burned out. Why not just do contract work? Just write motions on a contract basis. Then, you don't have that connection to the stress piece of the work. It's not your client, your deadline. You're just doing something you know you do well. And while it may not be completely purpose-driven, it may allow you to live another purpose, which could be more time with your family," he shared.

There is no shame in taking a similar approach. If you need to dial back your work to focus on other priorities, and you can swing that financially, it's okay if your work is a bit uninspiring. In fact, sometimes, the quest to find work that is inspiring can prevent us from taking necessary small steps forward. Instead of acting, we wait, and wait, and wait some more for the thing that feels *right*. Yet before we know it, years have passed, and we've done nothing, changed nothing.

The key, however, is to ensure that you have purpose *somewhere* in your life. "Your work can be devoid of purpose," Matt said, "as long as you're drawing it from somewhere else."

Reflection Questions

How do you define meaning in your life? Your career?

What does a meaningful, purposeful life look like to you?

Where do you find meaning in your life right now?

If you feel that your life is lacking in meaning in some way, what are some ways you can infuse more meaning into your life? Into your work?

Action Step

Write out several broad categories into which you can divide all of your activities. For most people, it will be something like "work," "relationships," "family," "wellness," and "service." Under each category, write down all the ways you're finding meaning in each.

Pay attention to which categories are the thinnest, as this can lend valuable insight into your quality of life. For instance, little meaning in the "family" or "relationships" category may signal a bigger, more chronic issue than a thin "work" section. If you find your work meaningful but your personal relationships are starving for your time and attention, reflect a bit on whether this is a sustainable long-term setup, even if it's fulfilling a very important short-term need.

CHAPTER 20
Don't Nail the Coffin

"If you don't see a door opening or a way to get closer to where your insides are telling you that you need to be, then talk to somebody. Get in motion. It will work out. But you've got to get going."

I have a friend who recently left a two-decade career as a law firm partner to take a career pause. She recently had her first child, a daughter, and chose to temporarily stay at home with her. Over coffee recently, she told me that when she gave her notice at her firm, she was shocked by the number of female senior partners who casually said, *oh, I did that too!* Even more pleasantly surprising was the multitude of women who assured her that the law would "still be there" when she was ready to return and that she should "enjoy this time" because children don't stay small forever.

I, too, have seen women lawyers take a career pause for a host of reasons. Can they step right back into their previous positions the moment they return to the workplace? Probably not. But can they break back into the legal field in *some* way, shape, or form?

Absolutely.

If this is true, why is it that so many lawyers, particularly women, resist leaving the law for fear that if they do, the door will slam shut and they can never again re-enter?

I call this the "nail-in-the-coffin" fallacy: the idea that if you leave the law for a J.D.-preferred position, or if you take time away from the workforce, you can never transition back into traditional legal practice. You'll lose your edge, your connections, your knowledge, your skill. But if law firms and corporations hire graduates fresh out of law school with no experience, then surely, they'd also hire a seasoned professional who took an intentional detour along the way.

"I'd Learned that the Law is Portable."

Jay Reeves is a writer, coach, and the founder of Your Law Life, a company that helps lawyers enhance their purpose, profits, and peace of mind through one-on-one consultations, retreats, live presentations, and special projects. Jay's career is a testament to the versatility of the law degree. With each of his several career pivots, Jay molded his work to fit the needs of his family and life season. He moved into his current line of work as a speaker, writer, and life coach at age 50.

Jay launched his legal career as a staff attorney for Legal Aid in Charleston, South Carolina. His work was deeply satisfying and he quickly learned that "the law can be a powerful source of goodness." But when his wife landed a post-doc position in Chapel Hill, North Carolina, it became clear that substantial change was afoot. This was simply not an opportunity their family could pass up.

This didn't faze Jay. "I'd learned that the law was portable," he said. Their family uprooted and moved to North Carolina. In a whirlwind of moving, switching careers, and having multiple babies in just a few years, Jay found a home with the legal news publication *North Carolina Lawyers Weekly*, where he worked as an editor. "One of my passions was reading and writing," he said. So, a position as legal editor was squarely in his wheelhouse, even though it looked nothing like his previous role representing indigent litigants in South Carolina. Yet Jay explained that none of his Legal Aid experience was wasted.

"My background was crucial to getting the job in the first place. And it made me better at the job," he told me. "The law is useful even if what you're doing isn't directly related to representing clients and going to court."

Indeed, being refined in the fires of law school, Bar Exam preparation, and the early years of legal practice shapes us into people who are incredibly adept at picking up new skills and adapting to unfamiliar environments. Shifting from litigation to editing a state-wide legal publication, for instance, is not as much of a stretch as it might initially seem. After all, a young lawyer who can handle a massive case volume and juggle unforgiving litigation deadlines can certainly handle an editorial calendar.

After his stint at *Lawyers Weekly*, Jay went on to serve as the Vice President of Risk Management at North Carolina Lawyers Mutual, the longest-standing legal industry insurance provider that covers more than 8,000 lawyers state-wide. In this role, Jay continued writing, speaking, and working with a legal-facing audience, though the role was drastically different from his editorial work. "It didn't make any sense," he said. "I'd always told people I would never wear a necktie. Then suddenly, I was working at Lawyers Mutual and wearing really nice ones." As unlikely as it was, though, the role worked for Jay's life stage and his family's needs. "Never say never," he said.

But when his life circumstances again demanded a shift, Jay left Lawyers Mutual to open his own law practice representing lawyers who faced disciplinary actions brought by the North Carolina State Bar. And after a few years, when his circumstances shifted again, he moved into his current role as a coach, speaker, writer, and consultant, which, in many ways, is the confluence of all of his past roles and experiences.

"I'm able to draw on all the strands," Jay said. At both Legal Aid and Lawyers Mutual, as well as in his own practice, Jay witnessed the many ways the law can save people when they are at their very worst. He has brought this perspective to his coaching and consulting work. "Nothing shocks me now," he said.

Jay's career proves that the law is, indeed, a very pliable and portable profession. He went from practicing, to writing and editing, to serving as in-house counsel, to private practice yet again, and all of these pivots have led him to his current position: the one that he calls "the best decision I've ever made." Each time, he was faced with a massive decision. First, it was leaving Legal Aid to follow his wife's career. Then, it was taking a role that paid well while his family was growing. Then, it was seeking the flexibility of solo practice, and finally, it was the adventure of entrepreneurship. Each time, these pivots worked out in Jay's favor, even though each one seemed like a hard left turn.

Jay's call to lawyers who might be feeling conflicted about their next career move is simple: "Calm down," he said. "Accept that you are in conflict (if that's the case). Focus on your feelings. Lawyers aren't good at that. If you don't see a door opening or a way to get closer to where your insides are telling you that you need to be, then talk to somebody. Get in motion. It will work out. But you've got to get going."

Reflection Questions

Are you worried that if you leave your current job, you'll burn a bridge with the legal profession? If so, what makes you feel this way? Has this fear been preventing you from pivoting?

Do you believe that if you built a successful legal career once, you could do it again? Have there been other times that you reinvented yourself or your career?

Are you willing to keep the "back door" to legal practice open by maintaining your license? What will this require of you? Are you willing to make that investment of your time, money, and energy?

If you plan to eventually circle back to a more traditional legal career, are you willing to start from a lower rung than the one you are leaving? Are you willing to try out a different practice area? Are you ready to be a beginner again and lose some of your current status in the legal profession?

Action Step

Do you know anyone in your circle who's taken time off from legal practice, whether to stop working altogether or to do something non-traditional? Reach out to this person to see if you can meet to discuss their career path. Ask them how they transitioned back into the law after taking a break.

Ideally, speak to as many people as possible who have done this so you can see patterns. Ask specific questions: What did their careers look like when they returned? Did they do anything specific in their time off to ensure they left the door to legal practice ajar?

CHAPTER 21
Let the Sunk Costs Sink

"Was it worth staying unhappy, mired, and misaligned in the name of 'using your degree?'"

In economic parlance, a "sunk" cost is money that's been spent and is unrecoverable. There's something about human nature that makes people hesitant to abandon an endeavor when they've already spent unrecoverable funds on it. Also, it can be about more than just money: a sunk cost can involve "sweat" equity like time, effort, and personal sacrifice. Even for those who were lucky enough to earn a scholarship, law school involves all three.

Because of this, many lawyers stay rooted in a traditional legal job instead of pivoting for fear of "wasting" the time, money, and political capital they spent on earning their degrees. *Why*, they ask, *would I stop practicing law when I worked so hard to earn my degree?*

In a J.D.-adjacent field, your law degree and legal experience are still essential, even if you aren't arguing motions in court or working in-house. And even if you leave the legal field, your degree will prove valuable in innumerable ways.

You can think on your feet.

You can parse contracts.

You can spot risk.

You can work under tremendous pressure.

You can quickly read, digest, and interpret reams of complex material.

You can analyze an issue from multiple angles.

You can find answers to difficult questions.

Even if you pivot into a job that you could have landed without a law degree, ask yourself if it was worth staying unhappy, mired, and misaligned in the name of "using your degree." Not to mention, the decades-older version of yourself is likely going to be much better at that job than you would have been as a 22-year-old. And after being stuck in a career that made you miserable, you will not take that job for granted as you might have otherwise.

A Deeply-Entrenched Limiting Belief

Erin Gerner, a mindset coach for women lawyers, describes the sunk cost fallacy as an intensely damaging and limiting mindset. In her work, she frequently encounters women who espouse a scarcity mindset around money in particular. "But our mindsets about money," she explained, "can hold us back." Erin explained that those who fear leaving the profession, or pivoting into a different industry niche, because they think they're wasting their education might find themselves reinforcing that damaging narrative. Conversely, those who trust that they'll figure out another way to earn money and return their investment will develop the tenacity needed to do just that.

Instead of fearing that you're wasting your education, time, and money, Erin said: "Tell yourself, *yes. I invested this money. But with patience and commitment to this pivot, I will earn it back. Possibly even in spades.*"

Reflection Questions

How did your legal education shape you not just as a lawyer, but as a *person?*

Think about other times in your life you've stayed in the same situation instead of pivoting because you feel you've already invested "so much" in that endeavor. Maybe it's something as serious as a failing relationship, or as simple and seemingly silly as a road trip gone sour.

- In these situations, did you stay the course or pivot?

- If you pivoted, how long did you feel the pain of the sunk cost?

- If you stayed the course, how did you feel?

- Did you ever wish you'd pivoted earlier or were you glad you stayed the course?

- Do you feel that situation is analogous to your current professional dilemma? If so, what makes them similar, and if not, what makes them different?

Action Step

It's time to shift your paradigm. Instead of thinking about what you might lose from pivoting, instead, ask yourself what you will gain. It's okay if the only thing that comes to mind is *less stress or peace.* That really does mean something.

Instead of fixating on the past or hand-wringing about whether you're on the right track, ask yourself what life could be like if you gave yourself permission to pivot *right now.* Write out a vision (not a plan, but a *vision*) for your future and get as granular as possible: What do you see? Where are you living? Working? What types of activities make up your days? Who are you sharing life with, whether family, friends, colleagues, clients, or others?

If you like the idea of creating a vision board, try that. Or you can journal, write out a "mind-map," or simply discuss your vision with someone you trust.

CHAPTER 22
Dismantle Your Five-Year Plan

"Embrace doing things differently. Just because law school taught you one way to do things, that's not necessarily the best way."

When interviewing for jobs, many professionals are asked to share their five-year plans. It seems from the beginning, we're stamped with the belief that we must have a plan, and then we fixate on said plan and funnel our energy into executing it as perfectly as possible.

The only problem is that plans tend to fall apart. A lot.

One of the most surprising insights I gained while researching for this book came from Davina Frederick of Wealthy Woman Lawyer, who we met in the first chapter. She told me that years ago, she stopped creating a five-year plan. When asked why, she would say that she did not set a plan because she didn't know what opportunities would be available to her in five years. So, why limit herself based on incomplete knowledge of what options she may have in her pocket by then?

This mindset fits the legal field well, given the continuing and rapid change affecting the industry. Technology is revolutionizing the practice of law, from unbundling legal services to introducing interdisciplinary approaches to resolving disputes. Several of the lawyers featured in this book are currently working in jobs that did not even exist a decade ago.

That said, if you cannot stop yourself from writing a plan, do it, but hold it loosely. Stay curious and receptive, open to the opportunities that might spring from the most unexpected experiences, encounters, or evolutions.

The private sector executive we met a few chapters ago shared exactly when, and how, his own five-year plan fell apart. In 2013, he worked for a different corporation, and his plan was to become its General Counsel. But when his current organization recruited him, he said: "I had to ask myself if I wanted to put aside that goal. I did, and I've never been happier." In his new role, he has not only helped his company grow, but he's become a global leader in his industry. He's made an impact that never would have been possible had he fixated on his original plan.

"It was almost a no-brainer," he said. "I thought, this makes perfect sense. This is what I need to do next. The dream of becoming a general counsel was an old dream. And what I realized was that *I* had changed."

It's not just about the industry changing or new opportunities arising. You need to give *yourself* permission to change, and then stay acutely aware of where your interests are leading you. Breaking up with an old dream can be hard, but if your pivot is the right choice, you won't grieve for long.

The Power of the Unconventional Plan

Colin Levy is a prime example of the ways pursuing our personal interests can feed our careers—in some cases, much more than adherence to a rigid plan. Colin is the Director of Legal and Evangelist for Malbek, a leading contract lifecycle management company. He also serves as an advisor for Proxy, a legal workflow management platform. But he is best known publicly for his writing and speaking on issues surrounding legal technology and the ways it is transforming the industry.

When he graduated from law school, Colin knew he didn't want to work for a large law firm (this was partially informed by his work as a Big Law paralegal before entering law school), but he didn't necessarily have a plan other than eventually jumping to an in-house position. But instead of taking the expected track for in-house hopefuls, which involves working at a law firm for a few years first, Colin took on a number of temporary roles that would give him the experience and skills he would need in the type of role he ultimately wanted.

After a few years, a technology company hired Colin to work in-house, which, in turn, ignited his interest in legal tech. "This little taste really stuck with me," he said. He realized that he wasn't the only one: there were many in the legal field who were hungry to learn more about technology and how it could shape the future of the industry, so he started to blog about what he was learning.

In building and growing his online presence, Colin interviewed leaders in the tech space and shared their thoughts on his blog. He also harnessed Twitter and LinkedIn to not only share his content, but also, to connect with professionals who were interested in similar topics. This gave him incredible access to some of the most respected thought leaders in the legal industry. "This opened a lot of doors for me," Colin told me.

The slightly unconventional route Colin took to in-house work, writing, and speaking highlights the truth that there is not one ideal path. There are many different ways to accomplish a specific career goal, so long as we are willing to be creative and flexible.

"In law school, you're taught there's really only one way to do or think about things," Colin explained. "But embrace doing things differently. Just because law school taught you one way to do things, that's not necessarily the best way."

In Colin's case, the time-tested, conventional route of working for a law firm before even attempting to apply to in-house positions was not agreeable to him, but he still found his way to the type of work he wanted to do. At points, even that path shifted and changed, "sometimes rapidly," he told me. But detaching himself from a rigid plan made Colin flexible enough to make these shifts.

It can be challenging to know when we should be ready to change course and when we should stay rooted where we are. But Colin's advice is "to constantly ask yourself why." In other words, continually evaluate the rationale behind your decisions. "If you can do that," he said, "it can inform you of what steps you need to take."

Reflection Questions

Do you have a five-year plan? If so, when did you (officially or unofficially) create your plan? How does your life now look different than it did when you first made your plan? Is this plan based on an old dream?

Are you open to taking a detour if new opportunities present themselves? What criteria will you use to assess whether an opportunity is worth considering?

What is the "why" behind the career change you want to make? Do you think this "why" can change?

Action Step

Take some time to review your answers to the questions in the very first chapter, "Ignite Your Pilot Light." Think about your original answers in light of what you've learned from reading the stories and answering the reflection questions in this book. Given what you've learned about yourself, your options, and the legal profession, do you believe that you can create a new, more flexible plan for your career? Take a few moments to write out a thoughtful answer. Set it aside, and revisit it periodically. This will be an ongoing process of discernment and careful, prudent decision-making.

Conclusion

When I was contemplating my own career pivot, I travelled a spectrum of emotions, from fear to uncertainty to sheer exhilaration. Most of all, I worried about being irresponsible. Was I shooting myself in the foot by stepping out of traditional legal practice? What if I wanted to return to practice in a few years? Was it any good to keep up my CLEs if I wasn't practicing law? Could I really cut it as a business owner? What if my business failed? Was I lazy, naïve, or entitled for not wanting to practice law anymore? Was I throwing away my education? Would I still have a career when I was 40? 50? 60? Would I have enough money saved up to retire?

I worried about being impulsive. I worried about throwing away a good thing. I worried about coming off as whiny or privileged. I worried about financial ruin. I worried about what other lawyers would think of me. In case you couldn't tell, I spent an awful lot of time worrying when, instead, I could have been taking proactive steps toward personal and professional growth.

At risk of painting our entire profession with a broad brush, lawyers are typically not impulsive by nature. We tend to ruminate, cogitate, and hesitate instead of forging ahead on an uncharted path. This could be due, in part, to our training. Impulsivity isn't exactly a trait that clients seek in their lawyers. But I believe that part of it is likely how we're fundamentally wired: certain types of people gravitate toward the law. As a population, we're far more likely to hesitate than to act. We tend to be more conservative than brash. Thus, if we err on the side of *action* rather than *caution*, we will likely still wind up in a safe zone. We're unlikely to unwittingly throw ourselves off a proverbial cliff. A risk-averse person's risk is less risky than a *non-risk-averse* person's risk. A lawyer's risk probably isn't going to lead to bankruptcy or a homeless shelter.

If you are intelligent and driven enough to earn a law degree, then you're more than capable of putting safety nets in place as you prepare to pivot. So if you feel a pull into something different, whether it's starting a business or stepping into a new industry altogether, make the move before you grow increasingly comfortable staying rooted. Don't let yourself become inert. As the American essayist John Burroughs is credited with writing: "Leap, and the net will appear." (Needless to say, he was not an attorney. But still. His words are a clarion call to all of us, no matter our professional status.)

Gone are the days when pedigree and prestige define success. A partner track at a large law firm is no longer the most coveted position for an intelligent, ambitious attorney, and it's not necessarily the most lucrative. And frankly, even if it were, there's more to life than money and prestige. As lawyers, we are fundamentally public servants, no matter our job title. Whether through traditional legal practice, entrepreneurship, academia, humanitarian work, or any number of other paths, we have tremendous power to do great good and support and champion those around us. But when we stay stuck, miserable, and misaligned, we stymie our ability to fulfill our potential. We help no one by being martyrs.

As the theologian and scholar Howard Thurman is credited with saying: "Don't ask what the world needs. Ask what makes you come alive and go do it. Because what the world needs is more people who have come alive."

Now it's your turn. This is your permission slip: permission to figure out what makes you come alive. Permission to go do it.

Permission to pivot.

ABOUT THE AUTHOR
Alexandra Macey Davis

Alexandra Macey Davis is a lawyer, writer, and editor. After practicing civil litigation for a few years, she worked as a ghostwriter and content consultant for legal industry leaders. She now works as the managing editor of an online public policy journal, and on the side, she writes articles and essays for various online and print publications. She lives in Raleigh, North Carolina with her husband and two young boys.

www.alexandramaceydavis.com

Acknowledgements

It's a privilege to live a creative life, and it truly takes a village to make this type of project possible.

First and foremost, my husband, Jacob, was the lucky recipient of many a tearful phone call in my litigation days. He was the very first person who helped me believe that indeed, there are many paths, and he encouraged me to explore them all.

My parents, Ed and Laurie Macey, are true saints for putting up with my career drama for the past decade and my personal drama for the past three. I've never had better mentors and guides, and I'm grateful for the many ways they've modelled prudence and wisdom.

My former employers, Jason Miller and Jeff Monroe, were patient with me as I learned how to be a lawyer and gave me my very first taste of the depth and breadth of possibility for my legal career. They were also my first client when I started my business. That means that not just once, but twice, they trusted me when it was clear I had absolutely no clue what I was doing.

This book improved dramatically after wise and honest feedback from my team of beta readers—Aly, Jeff, John, Laura, Marissa, and Theresa—who generously offered their time, talent, and insight and reminded me that this work is valuable.

Finally, I wholeheartedly thank the nearly two dozen lawyers who provided an interview for this book, even the ones whose wise words do not appear in these pages. Each of them provided the very backbone of the wise counsel I've been privileged to retain, reflect upon, and share in this book. Thank you, also, for showing us what it looks like to boldly explore uncharted territory. Your stories will continue to inspire and empower other lawyers to enjoy the breadth of opportunity our incredibly versatile degree gives us.

End Notes

i. Cameron, Julia. *The Artist's Way: A Spiritual Path to Higher Creativity.* New York: Penguin Random House, 1992.

ii. Fulwiler, Jennifer. *Your Blue Flame: Drop the Guilt and Do What Makes You Come Alive.* Zondervan: 2020.

iii. "2020 Law School Student Loan Debt." American Bar Association Young Lawyers Division. 2020. https://www.americanbar.org/content/dam/aba/administrative/young_lawyers/2020-student-loan-survey.pdf.

iv. Goins, Jeff. *Real Artists Don't Starve: Timeless Strategies for Thriving in the New Creative Age.* New York: Harper Collins, 2017.

v. https://academy.hubspot.com/courses/inbound-marketing

vi. There are ample resources available to guide you through applying for public service loan forgiveness (PSLF). Here is one that may serve as a starting point: https://thecollegeinvestor.com/22857/public-service-loan-forgiveness/#tab-con-9.

vii. Weikle, Brandie. "Millennials are on a quest to find meaningful work: And they're willing to take less pay to get it." CBC News, March 30, 2019. https://www.cbc.ca/news/business/millennials-meaningful-work-1.5075483.

Resources

Here are a few resources to help you discern your own pivot. Keep in mind that the resources on alternative J.D. careers will continue to shift and change, so this list is meant to serve only as a starting point and a springboard. I encourage you to remain hungry and curious about the opportunities that are continually developing in our industry.

Berkley Law School
Berkeley Law has compiled a comprehensive list of books, pamphlets, and courses on non-traditional J.D. careers. The full list is available on their website at: https://www.law.berkeley.edu/careers/other-resources/external-job-search-resources/alternative-careers/

National Association for Law Placement (NALP)
NALP has compiled a handout with valuable information about non-traditional J.D. career options. Check it out at: https://www.nalp.org/studentalumnihandouts

The American Bar Association

Visit the ABA website to access a database of articles and webinars on non-traditional J.D. careers: https://www.americanbar.org/careercenter/alternative-legal-careers/

Books

- *Alternative Careers for Lawyers* by Hilary Mantis

- *Lawyer Interrupted* by Amy Impellizzeri

- *Life after Law* by Liz Brown

- *Reversed in Part* by Adam Pascarella

- *What Can You Do with a Law Degree?* by Deborah Arron

Conferences

- Clio: https://cliocloudconference.com/

- ABA Tech Show: https://www.techshow.com/

- CLOC Global Institute: https://cloc.org/

- LegalWeek: https://www.event.law/legalweek

- ILTACON: https://www.iltacon.org/home

PIVOT